Calling All Workers

The Harvest Is Ripe, the Worker Is You!

By Michelle E. Caswell

aBM

Published by:
A Book's Mind
PO Box 272847
Fort Collins, CO 80527
www.abooksmind.com

ISBN: 978-1-939828-25-5

Printed in the United States of America

Dedication

To my First Love, Savior, and Healer.
You chose me at my worst, so now I live to be my best for You.
I pray that this book brings You tons of glory,
because You deserve it all!

To my amazing husband, you were so worth the wait.
Thank you for having my back through this journey of life.

To my kids…you inspire me to be better. I love you like crazy!
Here's to you.

TABLE OF CONTENTS

AUTHOR'S STORY

I grew up a wild child with huge dreams.... I wanted to be a counselor or a professional barrel racer and ride in rodeos like my dad, who was a calf roper. I wanted to be the rodeo queen—carrying the American flag on my horse, and racing around the arena with the crowd cheering as they stood to their feet and placed their hands over their hearts while the national anthem played.

I rode horses almost every day when I was little—practicing for the "big day," wearing my pink dance-leotard. Yes, I said pink dance-leotard. Every time I fell off, my dad was quick to say, "Dust yourself off, and get back on the horse." Now that might sound cruel to some, but it taught me to be tough—not to let anything knock me down and keep me down. It was a lesson I needed for the times ahead, not just for riding.

I started my first "business" when I was six. My best friend and I started a candy shop out of her playhouse—we did chores to make money, and then took that money to the little store to purchase "penny candy." By the time we opened our store, the candy had gotten old, so that didn't work so well. My second business was making homemade perfume out of the lilac tree in our yard. We took five-gallon buckets filled halfway with water, put in the flowers, and then began stepping on the petals with our feet—like how they make wine in the old country. I didn't make it very big in either of those businesses, but that never stopped me from trying. I always had high aspirations, and was told to get my "head out of the clouds" on many occasions.

My parents were practicing Christians at the time, and had my little sister and I in Godly environments regularly. I developed a really good relationship with Jesus—I always knew He was there. We would hang out together, talk, and play. I used to make up songs to Him.

Train up a child in the way she should go; even when she is old she will not depart from it.

— *Proverbs 22:6* (*pronoun change mine*)

At the young age of six, all Hell broke loose in my home; things moved from good to really bad—*fast*. I remember sitting in the back seat of the car. My mom's new boyfriend was driving, and my mom was in the passenger seat with my little sister in between them. My big strong cowboy dad was sitting on the front porch of our house with his head in his hands, and his body shaking from crying. I tricked myself into believing that divorce meant *moving*, so we were on our way to our new two-story yellow house in the country, and my dad was going to follow us and meet us there. I can still see that imaginary house in my mind. When my mom left my dad, we left our home, our horses, our bunnies, our dog and cat, my best friend, and our church. My whole life changed in a moment. I vowed never to make any of the same choices she made.

Overnight, I changed from a happy, outgoing, funny, dreamer—who was a daddy's girl—to a scared, sad, angry, rebellious child. My mom transformed from a stay-at-home mom who rode horses and went to church all the time, to an alcoholic who worked two jobs, and had a lot of men in her life. God was absent; she got as far away from Him as possible. My dad went from a present daddy, to a very distant dad; we went from seeing him every day…to every other weekend…to occasional afternoons and holidays.

I know now that they both played their part, but at the time, I blamed my mom for everything. I knew it was wrong, and I made sure to tell my mom *over* and *over* again. That decision set my feet on a path away from the Lord, and all that He stood for. However, I never stopped talking to Him and I never stopped hearing Him, but I was angry—because, in my opinion, He was the one who could have stopped it, but didn't.

When a good girl gets put in a bad environment, the girl turns bad. *Bad company corrupts good character* (1 Corinthians 15:33 NIV). Around the age of seven, was the start of being molested. I started cussing, smoking at 12, shoplifting, fist fighting, bullying others, and really messing around with boys. When I turned 14, it was another big year for me—I was raped as a virgin, was kicked out of the house, and started drinking and using drugs. All this happened the year I gave my heart to Jesus and got saved—however, my life didn't change; it got worse. I wanted to be a virgin when I got married. I wanted to have a normal life. A normal family. But that's not what I got.

After the rape occurred, I got even angrier and chose never to be a victim again. Instead, I became a predator, which led me to becoming a sex addict. Everything I said I *never* would be—I became—and then some. I became a teenage mom, a drug addict for 16 years, an alcoholic, a two-time divorcee, had two abortions, and was on state assistance—the more I focused on my anger and all the things I wouldn't become, the worse I got. The more I tried to get good, the more bad choices I made. I had absolutely zero understanding about the grace of God; I had no idea that *He* could make me good, and I had no chance at accomplishing it on my own.

After hitting rock bottom *again*...the Lord began to bring powerful women into my life. They mentored me out of my horrific lifestyle, and poured hope into me—*I could live a different life*. I chose to go to a Christian rehab, and I finally decided to give my *entire life* to Jesus. There's a huge difference between giving your *life* to Jesus and only giving your *heart*. Over many years, I took the steps needed to heal from the traumas in my past. I am happy to report that I have never backslidden into drugs, and I remained celibate for almost seven years prior to marrying my husband.

The Lord told me that I would be a leader of leaders, and that is the direction of this ministry. I have not appointed myself, rather the Lord has appointed me. I started at ground zero, and the Lord has continued to raise me up to leadership positions. Now He's calling me to teach others what has been taught to me. The revival has started in my own heart, and now I'm compelled to start a revival in people's hearts everywhere I go.

I believe that the way I healed was effective and long lasting and gave me a huge passion for mentoring, which I do so out of my own story of healing and the power of the Holy Spirit. My story has given me authority with those I'm called to. As I looked over the process of mentoring that I have done, I noticed there were five dynamic steps I would take them through. These steps are amazingly effective and I am about to share them with you.

I went to a Christian rehab to get the initial healing that I needed, and was raised up to become Head Staff which was second to my Director. After a year and a half, I left there and got a job at a Christian ranch for single moms and fatherless kids. There, I became the Women's Minister, working with every woman living there—which was upwards of 30 women—and all the women who visited, which was around 400.

After four years, I left there and began working at the church that had been used to save my life. I was the ministry and event coordinator. This included teaching Bible studies to the youth, and counseling women and girls through trauma and difficult times.

I have shared my story on countless church stages, ministry banquets, and now through my blog and this book. The Lord has been so good to me; He has redeemed me, and set me free from every addiction. He has restored my mind, healing me from all my mental disorders. I have over eight years clean and sober. He has firmly placed my feet on solid ground, and I will not be moved—because He is in me, and has full reign to do whatever He wants through me.

About two years into my healing, the Lord spoke to me and said, "Michelle, I am giving you back EVERYTHING that Satan stole from you. EVERYTHING." He has been true to His word—I even got my *innocence* back. Imagine that. I have been blessed with forgiveness from my boys, and a good relationship with both of them, as well as a restoration of my relationship with my parents who are both clean, sober, serving God again, and present in my life. I have also been extremely blessed with a godly husband whom I absolutely adore, and two stepdaughters who I love very much. I've gotten more back than I knew was stolen.

Several years ago, I started a ministry within a ministry called the Sisterhood: I mentored upwards of 17 Girls, ranging from ages 13-52. We met nearly five days a week, all together in my home, or sometimes outside when it was sunny. We were on a journey of becoming Purely His together through Bible teachings, encouragement, and accountability. We learned together, served together, and healed together. The relationships that were formed were real and lifelong.

The Lord gave me a vision one year before starting that group: the Girls would get to a place where they were healed enough to go back into their neighborhoods and into their circle of influence and start similar groups, and the process would just keep repeating itself—*disciples making disciples making disciples*. I pictured several of us telling our stories on a large stage, the audience full of women being mentored and mentoring. Breakout sessions would take place for different struggles, led by women who were set free from that particular struggle and understood. The women would receive more healing, hope, and freedom. I also pictured a website where a Girl who wanted to be mentored could put her zip code in and find a group to belong to.

I was so excited about the dream that the Lord had given me; I immediately started making plans. Someone in leadership, however, told me that my dream was from Satan, and anything that took me away from my current ministry was not from God. My heart was crushed, my excitement was crushed—and although I didn't agree or believe this leader, I was taught in rehab to obey my leaders as unto the Lord, so I did. I learned a lot from this man, some good ways of doing things, and some wrong ways of doing things, but that's another story entirely.

Fast-forward a few years, just months after I got married in 2012. I was with my mentor, friends from church, and my son at a Hillsong concert in Portland, Oregon. I decided to tell my mentor about the dream God had placed in my heart so many years before, because it was bubbling to the top again, and I wanted to pursue it. I thought that she might agree with what that leader in the past had said, but her response was quite the opposite: "You should TOTALLY do it Michelle. God put that dream in your heart a long time ago, and He has brought it to the surface again."

I could barely contain my enthusiasm…okay I *didn't* contain it at all. "THANK YOU LORD!" The music started, and it was the song "The Stand." As tears streamed down my face, I said, "I'll do it Lord. I'll do it, no matter how afraid I am of someone stopping me again."

He replied, "NO ONE will stop the plans I have for you. NO ONE."

I told Him, "I'm ready to share the stage now, Lord." Before, I had viewed myself as a *loser* for so long, I had become prideful when God healed me and granted me success in ministry with women. The success was so fulfilling, I wanted the glory all to myself, which I now know is totally wrong. When I said I was ready to share the stage I had no idea that my husband would someday be on that stage with me.

About a year after we started the nonprofit ministry, Purely His, Inc., my husband started feeling led to be a part of what we were doing—to take on the men's side of our ministry. Yes, I said the MEN'S side of our ministry. It is the delight of my heart to work in ministry with my husband—and hopefully the rest of my family at some point, that's my prayer anyway.

One of the greatest lessons I have learned through founding this ministry is "Do not put God in a box." I thought this ministry was going to be by women and for women, but the Lord had a different plan. Purely His is a Christian mentoring ministry for men AND women of all ages and backgrounds. It is for anyone wants to choose to go "all-in" with Jesus, and desires to get "un-stuck" from anything that stands in the way of a lifestyle of complete surrender to HIS calling.

I felt alone most of my life. Looking back, I wish someone had taken me by the hand sooner to show me how to live like a Christian. How much heartache would I have been saved from? I believe very strongly in the power of mentoring—through authentic relationships. I have been mentored, and continue to be mentored, by women who know Jesus and make Him known to me. They continuously point me back to Him, and I do the same for others. I heard a really good quote once: "He gave His all for me, so I'll give my all for Him." God has saved me and set me free from so many things; I want others to experience the same freedom and joy I now have. I am absolutely compelled to help others in ways that I have been helped. My desire is to connect those who are alone and hurting to the one who promises to NEVER leave them—*Jesus*.

Thanks for reading my story. Now, let me share with you how I mentor. I hope it helps.

Sincerely,

Michelle

This book is for both men and women to read. To keep the reading smooth and simple, all pronouns used are for women. Men, you have not been forgotten, but you will have to read yourself into it though.

Chapter 1—The Harvest & the Worker

Jesus went through all the towns and villages, teaching in their synagogues, proclaiming the good news of the kingdom and healing every disease and sickness. When he saw the crowds, he had compassion on them, because they were harassed and helpless, like sheep without a shepherd. Then he said to his disciples, "The harvest is plentiful but the workers are few. Ask the Lord of the harvest, therefore, to send out workers into his harvest field."

— *Matthew 9:35-38*

The Harvest

Everyone needs a friend. Too many people feel alone in this world, just like you probably did at one time. Since the beginning of starting Purely His, I've been asking the Lord, "What do you want us to do?"

The Lord keeps saying, *"The harvest is ripe, but the workers are few. Go after the workers."*

There is no shortage of people wanting and needing help, but there is a huge shortage of workers. Won't you join me in rescuing the ones who need help? Let's face it, someone is harvesting, and it's not the Christian church. We need to be doing more.

Jesus is coming back soon—and I for one, don't want to waste the opportunity to do what He's called me to do. We can and should show our love to God by doing what He says which is *go into all the world and make disciples of all nations* (Matthew 28:19). Did He just say that to church leaders or pastors? No. He commanded all of us to do it. God says, *"If you love Me, keep my commands,"* (John 14:15).

I live in a valley in southern Oregon. Of the 223,000 who live here, 173,000 self-identify as not being connected to any Christian church. Now that is a ripe harvest!

I believe we should raise up workers from within the Harvest. Who better to reach a drug addict than a former addict? Who better to reach someone going through a battle of cancer than someone who has gone through the same thing? If you have a heart for a certain type of person, then my suggestion is to go reach someone who comes from that background—and watch them effectively reach that group of people.

Don't you wish someone would have come into your life sooner and helped you walk a new way? Who was it that God used to do that? Wouldn't it be awesome to be that person for someone else?

We all need support—whether who choose to lead a group, or mentor one-on-one. In fact, I believe we as mentors and leaders need the most help, because for some reason we think we SHOULD have it ALL together. The truth is—none of us do. Plus, the more we pour out, the more we need to be filled up.

The benefits of seeing and watching someone reach their full potential in Christ is absolutely amazing. There is nothing like it. For instance:

> *I met one of my Girls when she was nineteen. She dressed in gothic-type clothing, her head was shaved, and she wore a spiked dog collar—yes, I said a dog collar. She was addicted to the attention of men, was very rebellious and full of bitterness. Six years later, she's been single and serving Jesus for all those years. She volunteers a lot of her time mentoring young women, her hair is long, and she dresses very girly now—no sign of bitterness is left on her face. She is free!*

Why am I so passionate about this? Because Jesus is passionate about it. It is missing in our churches and the aftercare programs in our communities. Statistics show that most people aren't successful long term. They make it for a while, and then they backslide. The women and men who have someone walking through life with them-make it. They are able to stay clean, sober, and out of destructive relationships. There is a major shortage of Christians who are working WITH the Lord to truly help others.

People feel alone even in a crowd. It's time that we bond together the way that God designed us to. We are stronger together than we are apart. Too many people are feeling alone in this world. We need to take our rightful place in our families, communities, and churches.

Find Someone to Mentor

There is NO shortage of people who need or want mentoring; it's the mentors that are lacking. Here are a few ways for you to find someone who want to be mentored.

Tell Your Story: My favorite and most effective way is telling my story one-on-one, or in large groups. As soon as someone hears that I can relate to them—or have been through something they are currently going through—they automatically feel comfortable that I won't judge them, and that I know what I'm talking about. It gives me instant credibility. This is the best way that I've found. This also opens the door for family members and friends of those who are struggling to recommend me as a mentor.

Talk to Your Church Leadership: Church leaderships are generally bogged down with mentoring, and desperately need help. Tell them your story and the kind of people you relate to best and watch the referrals come in.

Check Your Circle of Influence: The person you're looking for is most likely already in your circle of influence; she might be way on the outside, but she's there. Look around at your daughter's friends, a co-worker, or the woman alone in the back row of the church who slips in and slips out.

Volunteer at a Local Mission: You can offer your assistance at a homeless shelter, pregnancy resource center, become an abuse recovery teacher, or offer to lead a Bible study at church.

Become a Purely His Mentor: Take advantage of our advanced training, and we'll put you on our list of available mentors. We get calls all the time from people needing a mentor. Read about it later in chapter 8.

Start a Purely His Mentoring Group: Advertise what you're doing, and people will come. Once the group attendees get pumped about it, word of mouth will take over from there, because they will not want their friends to miss out. You can start it in your home or church. Read about it later in chapter 8.

Determine Their Readiness

The most important thing to do is to determine if she is willing and coachable, because you can't help those who aren't. All you need to know is if they really want help and are willing to do what it takes to get it. There's no reason to force someone to get help when they really don't want it. Actions speak louder than words. She may say she wants help, but then doesn't show up to your meetings with her, or never follows through on your advice. That's called "giving you lip service." She is telling you what she thinks you want to hear.

Sometimes, we aren't the right fit for a person, and that's okay; find someone who might be able to relate better, and choose to step out of that mentor role. Now...don't use this as an excuse, because that mentee is hard to deal with or stretches you. I'm mainly saying this when you can tell very early on that you two are not a match made in Heaven.

The Worker

"Calling All Workers," you are an answer to my prayers…I have been asking the Lord to send out His chosen workers into the fields. The good news is *He has prepared good works in advance for you to do* (Ephesians 2:10). He already has assignments for you, so thank you for joining me as we serve the Lord alongside each other.

Our assignments will most likely be chosen for us according to our past experiences, giftedness, and hearts for different types of people groups. You are going to reach those that I can't relate to, and I'm going to reach those that you can't. Alone, we are weak—but together, we are going to be so strong! It's awesome to partner with you. I am

SUPER EXCITED because the kingdom of God is about to *grow*. We each have a circle of influence, now we just need to reach out to those that we have a heart for, and encourage them to go into their circle of influence and reach more people. That is how this movement will get going and keep going.

Thank you for saying "yes" to Jesus; together, we can flip this world upside down, one person at a time—just like the early disciples did. The Lord said that we would do greater things than Him, and that the way we show Him our love is to do what He commands:

> *... go and* ***make disciples*** *of all nations, baptizing them in the name of the Father and of the Son and of the Holy Spirit, and teaching them to obey everything I have commanded you. And surely I am with you always, to the very end of the age.*
>
> *—Matthew 28:19-20*

The awesome part about what He says there is that we aren't expected to make disciples on our own. Jesus is with us, and He is our helper. I'm guessing you've picked up this book, because you already are a "worker," and have probably found some great tools to help you along the way. I'm about to share with you the things that worked for me—and the things that didn't—whether it was through my own healing or through the healing of those I've mentored. I hope these **tools, tactics, and strategies** will help you do what you're already doing... better or more effectively. I do not claim to have all the answers, or the only way...I just know that these have worked for me, and for those I've been privileged to help.

Qualified to Mentor?

Jesus qualifies you. You don't need anyone else's permission.
Answer these questions:

1. Are you a follower of Christ?
2. Has He rescued you, forgiven you, and changed your life?
3. Are you an older woman (spiritually speaking that is)?

If you answered "Yes" to any of these questions, then you are qualified. Now, you just need to learn the skills to be *effective* and help those you have a heart for—versus hurting them further.

Teach the older men to exercise self-control, to be worthy of respect, and to live wisely. They must have sound faith and be filled with love and patience. Similarly, teach the older women to live in a way that honors God. They must not slander others or be heavy drinkers. Instead, they should teach others what is good. These older women must train the younger women to love their husbands and their children, to live wisely and be pure, to work in their homes, to do good, and to be submissive to their husbands. Then they will not bring shame on the word of God.

—Titus 2:2-5 (NLT)

In this scripture, there is a list of how we should be living—and therefore mentoring others to live the same way. Are you doing these things?

It doesn't matter what chronological age you are right now. You can still be considered and older woman spiritually. I am physically younger than several ladies I mentor, but spiritually I am older—or maybe just a little ahead of them in some area— therefore, it qualifies me to help them. There are areas that they mentor me as well.

Discipleship vs. Mentoring

I have found that people, in general, are intimidated by the word or concept of DISCIPLESHIP; we choose to use the word *mentor* to avoid that. Let's not get hung up on the word, but rather the concept.

What is Christian discipleship? By definition, a disciple is a follower of Christ who accepts and assists in the spreading of the good news of Jesus Christ.

What is mentorship? Mentoring is a relationship between an experienced person and a less experienced person for the purpose of helping the one with less experience. The mentee (one being mentored) seeks the advice and support of the more experienced person. Mentors answer questions concerning the tasks that their mentees need to succeed in reaching their goals. The mentor provides wisdom, guidance, and counseling as mentees advance their walk with the Lord.

CHAPTER 2 —GETTING PREPARED

Do your best to present yourself to God as one approved, a worker who does not need to be ashamed and who correctly handles the word of truth.

— 2 Timothy 2:15

First Things First

Make sure to keep your priorities in check. When you are really good at something, like mentoring or ministry, it is a natural tenancy to forsake our spouses and kids to do something where we get accolades and feel a sense of deep purpose. As a godly person and a mentor, it's important to keep our families as a very high priority, because they deserve our best, not our leftovers. This subject is very close to the Lord's heart:

*Likewise, teach the older women to be reverent in the way they live, not to be slanderers or addicted to much wine, but to teach what is good. Then they can **urge the younger women** to love their husbands and children, to be self-controlled and pure, to be busy at home, to be kind, and to be subject to their husbands, **so that no one will malign the word of God**.*

— Titus 2:3-5

Ministry is totally awesome, gratifying, and fun for me…however when I'm doing the Lord's work, I ask myself if it's in the Lord's way? Spouses often get jealous of Jesus and/or our ministry. If that is the case, then spend some real quality time to reassure him with your time, words, and involvement.

The Lord says that my spouse and children are my first ministry—in fact, when I minister to them first, then I can minister to others much better. In addition, those I mentor benefit from watching me do what the Lord requires of me.

Personal story:

I am very ministry-minded, and my husband met me like this. Knowing my tendency, I gave him permission to let me know when I'm doing too much. I have also given him permission to tell me when he doesn't want me to share something about our life or my past. I am such an open book, and so used to living a life of "dropping my mask and keepin' it real," which can make my husband nervous. So it is up to me to be sensitive to that. I blog parts of my story on our website purelyhisministry.com and some of the content is about my past sexual addiction, so there have been a couple of times that my husband asked me to change the wording.

In his words:

> *"I think it's important for you to share this part of your story so that women who are struggling can have hope of getting free. I would be fine with it if I knew that only women read this, but I know there are men who have the wrong intentions reading your blog, and I don't want them looking at you like that."*

I know it's my husband's job to protect me, so I submit to him as unto the Lord—and because I love him. Love is an action not just a feeling.

Mentoring from an Unhealthy Place

You hypocrite, first take the plank out of your own eye, and then you will see clearly to remove the speck from your brother's eye.

— Matthew 7:5

Save yourself—and everyone else—the heartache, and get healthy first. It's important that you go first. If you don't, then you could cause some serious damage to those you are "helping."

Christians in really hard situations turn to their mentors, churches and pastors for help. Some feel loved and accepted unconditionally; others walk away deeply wounded. It is a direct result of one of two things: the leaders not taking care of their own needs for healing first or they are mentoring from the flesh versus the full cup of the Spirit.

You get help first, and continue to have people who are bold enough speak into your life. The more you give—the more you need to receive. Stepping into ministry can really make you prideful, it can go straight to your head. It's a pitfall that we need to be aware of. I know…it happened to me. I was prideful and arrogant in my past and it just carried over into ministry. Be careful that you do not fall into that same trap, because *pride comes before a fall* (Proverbs 16:18).

Purely His mentoring groups are an incredible resource for you to be a part of first—before leading a group of your own. You can get the healing you need with things you didn't even realize were still unresolved, but are still affecting your life today. Plus, the authentic relationships built in the groups will help hold you accountable when you need it—and believe me, you will need it. Read more about this in Chapter 8.

Know Him as Savior First

The more you realize how much you have truly been forgiven for, the deeper you will be able to love. You are not any better than anyone else. We are all horrible sinners. The quicker you know that, the more deeply you can connect with the Lord and others. God knows how bad we are, how good we think we are, and He still chose us. God sees the end from the beginning. He saw all the sins you were going to commit, and He looked at you and said, "See that one? I'll take her as my own." *Let that one sink in a minute.*

God has so many names and titles, but you need to **know Him as your Savior** first, because the greatest commandment is *love*—and the key to experiencing that kind of love is realizing what you've been forgiven for.

Those who have been forgiven much, love much.

— Luke 7:47 (paraphrase of verse)

What have you been forgiven for? Reach into the depths of your painful past, and recount the things He has forgiven you for—in order for you to love better. This will also give you the joy of your salvation back! Keep in mind, it's important to look at your sin without downplaying it by comparing it to someone else's "worse" sin.

Real Life Example:

I had been in rehab for a few months at the time, and I remember holding onto the "fact" that I was a good person who happened to have a drug addiction. I mean, "Come on Lord...I would give my last cigarette, smoke my last bowl of marijuana with someone, make dinner for elderly neighbors, I was even nice when I turned a guy down who asked me to dance. I was a good person, and I still am."

I was trying to make myself not feel so bad. In fact, I was justifying my behavior to the Lord, while trying to convince myself that my "good deeds" could cancel out my sin. I wanted to hold onto some shred of self-esteem. That's when the Lord knocked me off my high horse and showed me my motives.

He said, "Look at the reasons that you chose to do those things for people...it was all about what they thought of you, not that you cared about them. You made dinner for those elderly women, because a guy was watching you—and you wanted him to think that you would be a good wife. Apart from me, you are nothing."

I doubled over, holding my stomach and bawling. I realized that I had absolutely nothing to offer, and there was no good in me. That's the day I really began to change. I was emptied of myself, and the Lord was able to start filling me back up with Him.

When you realize the sin in your own life—whether past or present—and recognize Jesus as your much-needed Savior, it will help you relate better to those the Lord calls you to work with, and will give you a deeper compassion for them. You don't have to have a super crazy testimony to have a deep understanding and appreciation for God's grace and how to love His people. You don't need to experience the exact same trauma or sin in your past to be able to empathize with someone's deep pain. However, when truly recognizing your own deep pains and horrible sin choices, you will be more equipped with compassion than if you don't allow yourself to go there. So GO THERE. Take some time with the Lord, and ask Him to remind you of all the things He's forgiven you for—and then begin to thank Him.

Too many times, we want to compare our sins to another, and decide for ourselves that their sin is worse than ours. That is *not* how the Lord weighs sin. You have been forgiven of so much, so take the time to recognize it, and watch the joy of your salvation return!

Therefore, I tell you, ***her many sins*** *have been forgiven—as her great love has shown. But whoever has been forgiven little loves little."*

— Luke 7:47 (emphasis mine)

Team Effort

Mentoring is something we do WITH the Lord. We are just vessels for Him to work through. All glory to Him. This is something we do WITH the Lord, not FOR Him. We are a team.

Those who unite themselves with Christ are one with Him in spirit. 1 Corinthians 6:17

It is a trap to take credit for the work of the Holy Spirit—because it feels so good to help or know the answers, especially if you were a loser like I was for so long. It's very important to mentor as unto the Lord—not yourself. Gently push her toward Him, His Word, and His opinions. For instance, "What has the Lord told you about that? What is He putting on your heart?" Push her to pray and seek Him *before she seeks you*. Teach her how.

Get to know Him as your partner in ministry and life. He has given us the Holy Spirit so that we have a Helper. He said that we would do greater things than He—and we can. We have His power in us, and we can have more of that same power if we are anointed by the Holy Spirit for service.

There is a difference between the Holy Spirit being *in* you and the Holy Spirit coming *upon* you—it's different degrees of power and ability. When you are sealed with the Holy Spirit on the inside, your salvation is secure; then He begins to sanctify you, making you new. When the Holy Spirit comes upon you, then you are prepared for service in ministry. If you haven't received this, then there is a very good chance that you are leaning on your own strength and power and are missing out on what could be.

It's rather simple to receive the anointing of the Holy Spirit. This process is for those that desire the anointing of the Holy Spirit, so they you can serve the Lord's people more effectively. Contact a few older brothers and sisters in the Lord to join you, as you lay down your entire will to the Lord, repent of all sin, and ask Him to fill you and prepare you for service. Meanwhile, the others are praying blessings over you and confirming what you are asking of the Lord. Just receive and believe that He has done it.

With Jesus

It's really important that we learn to mentor as part of a team with Jesus. Hurting people don't need more of us—they need more of Him. They need to hear the wisdom from Heaven, not of this world, so stay connected with Jesus while you're mentoring. Mentoring is something we do WITH Him, not FOR Him. We are just willing vessels for Him to work through. We are a team.

Sometimes, we can tend to take the glory for ourselves for the healing that happens in a person's life, versus giving it to the One who actually healed her. It's hard not to take the credit yourself when you see the fruit in their life, but He is actually the One who made the fruit grow in the first place. The Holy Spirit has been witnessing to them, and Jesus has been interceding for them day and night. You are just the privileged one He used to make it happen. It was His power that pulled it off though. He says that *he will share His glory with no man* (Isaiah 42:8). So let's do our best to give glory where glory is due. You will receive your reward in Heaven for allowing Him to use you here, so you can look forward to that.

Here's one way to respond when someone tries to give you all the glory for the change in someone's life, *Thank you, it's been a privilege to be used by the Lord in this way.*

The part I love about working with the Lord is that I get to see miracles happen in front of my eyes. People are set free from bondages that have held them captive for years—and it is gone in a *moment.* I also love knowing that I'm not in it alone; He is right there with me, protecting me, and guiding me.

With People

It takes a lot of different people to help a person get to a place of freedom in Christ. I have had the privilege of harvesting several people for the Kingdom, but there were many before me preparing that person prior to me getting to them. That's a hard one to remember because sometimes we like to think we're just that good. *Oh...am I the only one who struggles with that?*

A parent, spouse, child, or friend has been praying for them. They may have heard the word of God in some capacity—another mentor, a parent, or grandparent may have had influence. Remember that it is a collaborated effort in harvesting a crop of Believers.

I planted the seed, Apollos watered it,
but God has been making it grow.

— 1 Corinthians 3:6

Chapter 3—Do's & Don'ts of Mentoring

Relationship Is Key

Do make the relationship the most important part. Building a relationship with those you mentor is very important. It will give you both the right and permission to speak into their lives. This takes effort on your part by being as real and vulnerable as possible, so that you can connect on an authentic and deep level. *Newsflash: no one connects on superficial topics*. Jesus was very relational, so we should be following His example.

Bring them into your life. Invite them to follow you. Sound familiar? Bring them to a Bible study, company picnic, church event, even a birthday party for your kids. A lot of times, mentoring is just living life in front of, or with them. Your life is on display at all times, but living an authentic life in front of them is where you share your current struggles and not just things you have been set free from. It's allowing them to visit you in your home, see the interaction between you with your family, and watch how you live outside of a church environment.

Let it go beyond a mentoring relationship. A lot of the Girls I have worked with are like family to me now. It was a natural progression in relationship, and has huge benefits. Don't be surprised when they mentor you someday. If you do it right, they will.

Pour from a Full Cup

Do pour from a full cup. When you are pouring into others through mentoring, it should be coming from what has been poured into you. If we try to mentor when we are empty, then we end up giving them our self and that's not what they need—they need Jesus. When we're running on empty (running on fumes) we are in the flesh, not in the Spirit, and that is tiring. When you are full—it will feel easy, because it will just pour out of you. So do a favor for both yourself and the people you desire to help—*get filled up*. The more you give—the more you should be receiving. You cannot give what you do not have. So go get it, then you can give it away.

I know that we all have crazy-busy lives, and it's hard to know how to fit all of this in, but choosing to get empty and stay empty is not an option for me. My time is pretty full with mentoring, and it comes naturally when I'm in close relationship with the Lord. It overflows out of me.

Our number-one job is to get close to Jesus; the rest will come naturally.

The way I do this is by including Jesus in everything I do—including writing this book right now. I take seriously these two scriptures: *Pray without ceasing* (1 Thessalonians 5:17, ESV) and *Acknowledge the Lord in all your ways* (Proverbs 3:6, NET). He goes everywhere with me; so I am constantly talking to Him about everything that's going on—the good, the bad, and the ugly. My favorite times to talk to Him are in the shower, on a walk, watering the grass or flowers, and in the car. Those are the times I hear Him best. When is it for you?

Practical ways that I get filled up:

1. **CHURCH:** I attend a church service every week. It is never an option for me; it is always on my calendar.
2. **BIBLE STUDY:** I go to Bible studies or classes at church.
3. **BE ENCOURAGED and MENTORED:** I talk to at least one of my mentors a week about my own issues and get encouragement or prayer. I also have encouraging and straightforward godly friends who encourage me, but aren't afraid to call me out either. So I am getting mentored on a regular basis.
4. **PRAYER:** I pray every day.
5. **TIME SET ASIDE FOR HIM:** I do not have a special quiet time every morning at five…in my special chair, in my special spot. I know that method is taught by a lot of people, and I'm sure it

works for some, but it does not fit my personality at all. I prefer to go on walks with the Lord, and talk out loud to Him—or sit on my back porch and hang out with Him.

6. **PRAISE:** I sing a lot.
7. **MUSIC:** Listen to Christian music primarily (except on rare occasions when one of my sons wants to listen to Country or Dub Step). I have found a lot that I really enjoy, like alternative-rock Christian music.
8. **RELATIONAL BIBLE READING:** I read my Bible relationally, *trying to get to know Him better*, NOT because *that's what good Christian women do*.
9. **SHARING:** I recount my blessings over and over again—by telling my story through blogging and sharing with others personally, it reminds me that He is with me and for me. It also reminds me that He came through for me in that specific trial, so I know He'll do the same now.
10. **WORSHIP NIGHTS:** I attend a monthly night of worship and encouragement through a local ministry.
11 **RETREATS and SPECIAL EVENTS:** I attend special events throughout the year—like a women's retreats, Christian concerts, etc.
12. **BIBLE READING:** I read my Bible several times a week on my own—whether sitting on the back porch when it's nice out, or sitting in bed at night. I randomly choose one, or sometimes I'll ask the Lord which one I should read. Usually, I read until the Lord reveals a new truth to me—or until I get my answer. I may only read for five minutes, or just a couple paragraphs.
13. **SHARE WHAT HE IS DOING:** I write blogs or Facebook updates about what He's done in my life. It seems to remind me that *He is with me, and working on my behalf behind the scenes*. There is something about writing it down or sharing it verbally that cements it into my memory. I use my story a lot when I'm mentor-

ing, to show the Girls that I can relate or give a practical example of a scripture or a step that needs to be taken.

14. **LISTEN TO TAUGHT WORD:** I enjoy listening to sermons while I'm cleaning my house or taking a bath.
15. **FASTING:** Fasting is a great way to empty myself and allow Him to fill me back up. Most people fast from food, however there are many different things to fast from such as television, coffee or Facebook. **People in recovery from eating disorders should NOT use food fasting to honor the Lord until they are walking STRONGLY in their healing.**

I know this may seem like a lot of time that it takes for me to fill up, and maybe it is, but it seems easy to me now, because I have made a conscience effort to include Jesus in every part of my life. Plus, I love the emotional benefits from doing it. I feel so much better than I used to—when I was trying to do everything on my own. Basically, I surround myself with Jesus at all times. Making it easy for me to talk about Him and share Him with others, because He's fresh on my mind and in my heart; He's overflowing from me.

This is what works for me. Find what works for you and fits your personality. Then, share it with others. There is no perfect way to get filled up. God made us all unique for a reason...*so get creative.*

The main thing is to strategically put yourself in environments that support your growing walk with the Lord, and encourage you toward a more positive life where people hold you accountable—because you let them.

They Are Watching You

Do stay on your toes, because they are watching you.

Join together in following my example, brothers and sisters, and just as you have us as a model, keep your eyes on those who live as we do....

Whatever you have learned or received or heard from me, or seen in me—put it into practice.

— Philippians 3:17, 4:9

The women in my life that I mentor, keep me on my toes and constantly challenge me to walk out what I say I believe. I'm tempted sometimes to wear a mask—*so I look more spiritually mature than I am*—but I've chosen instead to "keep it real" with them. They don't expect me to be perfect. They like to look up to someone that makes them think "Boy, if she can do it, then I definitely can."

I live my life remembering that they are watching my every move. I need to be living right by keeping my eyes on Jesus—so they don't fall or think it is okay to live an ungodly life. This can feel like a lot of pressure, if you let it, but it's really not. All YOU have to do is *keep your eyes on Jesus* and continue growing in your relationship with Him. The concept is "follow me as I follow Christ." You're just bringing her along for the ride.

You don't have to be perfect. She doesn't want you to be—or expect that—but you should live a repentant life, and when new sins are brought to your attention, repent again. We need to practice what we preach. We mentor more with our life than we do with our words. Continue allowing the Lord to make your life worthy of following (Philippians 3:17-21).

The closer you get to Him—the farther you get from sin. When you start pursuing a relationship with the Lord, you are naturally moving toward holiness and righteousness and moving away from sinfulness. Keeping your eyes and attention on Him, draws you away from the things of this world. It's much easier than constantly fighting the temptation *not to sin* and focusing on the sinful behaviors and trying *not to give in*.

"Whatever you feed—grows, and whatever you starve—dies."

—Unknown

When you feed your spirit (godly nature) and starve the flesh (sinful nature), what happens? Your spirit gets stronger and your flesh gets weaker. One of the benefits to feeding your spirit is that you will naturally begin loving what He loves and hating what He hates. You will also be much stronger in the face of temptation, it won't be as alluring as it used to.

Vice versa, when you starve your spirit and feed your flesh, what happens? Your flesh gets stronger and your spirit weakens. When your flesh is strong, temptation is very difficult to resist and therefore, backsliding into your old lifestyle is almost inevitable.

The easiest way to do this is to move completely toward Jesus, and away from all that holds you back. Don't even focus on the sin, rather focus on the Lord. This is one of the ways to go "all-in" with Jesus.

...whatever is true, whatever is noble, whatever is right, whatever is pure, whatever is lovely, whatever is admirable—if anything is excellent or praiseworthy—think about such things.

— Philippians 4:8

We need to practice what we preach. We mentor with our lives. Just bring them along with you. They will follow you as you follow Christ.

A Mentor's Job Is

1. **LOVE:** It's the greatest commandment. People need love more than anything and all the following points are under the heading of **LOVE**.
2. **SERVE:** If you have a desire to become great, become a servant to those you mentor. Jesus came not to be served, but to serve—*copy Him*. In John 13, He even washed Judas's feet. He knew Judas was going to betray Him, but He loved him all the way till the end. It was Judas who left Jesus, not the other way around
3. **SEE:** See what God sees in them. Picture her already healed and being used by God. *Choose to see the end from the beginning*. This will give you hope and help you endure those times that feel hopeless. It will get you through the moments where you believe

there isn't any hope for them either. *There is—just like there was for you.*

4. **INSPIRE:** Paint a new dream of what their life could look like. Most people need hope; encourage them and speak hope into their hopeless lives. *Speak to the dry bones and raise up an ARMY*! (Ezekiel 37)
5. **ACCOUNTABILITY:** When she confesses a sin, or a struggle with sin, ask for permission to call her out if you see her being tempted to go back down that road again.
6. **ADVOCATE:** Stand up for her. People are always putting her down, and not believing in her. She is probably her own worst enemy; contradict the bad things she says about herself with the truth of what you see. Don't lie and give her false compliments—search out the God-given beauty.
7. **HOLD HER LOOSELY:** You are not in control of the outcome. We can only help those who truly want help and are ready to do what it takes to heal. Let them go, if they want to go. Read more about this in: "You win some, you lose some" in chapter 7.
8. **BE TRUSTWORTHY:** Love her enough to "keep it real." Don't ever lie, or you will lose her for good. People who have had a hard life are smarter than some give them credit; they are going to know if you are hiding something, or just telling them what they "want" to hear. Be brave, and spit it out in love. You will become the "go-to girl" if you earn their trust, and they will reach out to you when they really need the help.

A Mentor's Job Is Not

I have made a ton of mistakes, and a ton of mistakes were made on me—so learn from our mistakes.

1. **SAVIOR:** You cannot and will not save her. By surrendering your life to be used by Jesus, however, you become a vessel for the Holy Spirit to use you to save someone's life physically, emotion-

ally, and/or spiritually. This requires *intentionally surrendering* your life to the Lord on a regular basis.

2. **HOLY SPIRIT:** You are not there to convict her of her sin. That doesn't mean you can't call her out or bring attention to it, but don't continue to beat her with it. Let the Holy Spirit do His job.
3. **SEE LIKE JESUS:** You are not above or better than her, so don't compare your sin to hers even in the "privacy" of your mind. Something to help with this is to recount what the Lord has forgiven you for, and thank Him. We are to *consider others better than ourselves* (Philippians 2:3) and remember *the least of these will be greater in His kingdom* (Matthew 11:11). Ask the Lord to give you the eyes to see them the way that He does.
4. **HER REAL AUTHORITY:** Don't lord your authority over her. *Jesus gave His life as a ransom for many* (Matthew 20:28). Her authority is Jesus Christ—not you. She might look up to you and ask you for advice, but don't use that to Lord your authority over her or to micro-manage. Some mentors take their "authority" too far; if you do this, she will become afraid and begin avoiding you—plus, it gives little room for Jesus to be her true Lord.
5. **DOCTOR or COUNSELOR:** Be careful not to diagnose a person with any mental disorders. You can tell your own personal stories, but if a person suspects or has been told by others that they have a disorder or physical aliment, encourage them to see a doctor or counselor for further examination, or to be diagnosed. I mentor several people who also see counselors on the side, and we become a great team wrapping around them.
6. **DO NOT EVER PROMOTE SIN**, such as divorce. So many Christians are quick to promote sin and just go with what the world says, but the Bible strongly warns us:

If anyone causes one of these little ones—those who believe in me—to stumble, it would be better for them if a large millstone were hung around their neck and they were thrown into the sea.

— Mark 9:42

7. **TAKE ALL THE GLORY:** The glory belongs to the Lord for *any* healing and redemption that happens. Do your best to remember that and praise God for the part that He allowed you to play.
8. **EXPLOIT or GOSSIP:** Always ask for permission to share someone's story. Some people have gotten good at spiritualizing gossip.

   They will say things like:

   "We need to be praying for Suzie. She's fallen into sexual sin again with that boy she used to date."

   A better way to ask for prayer:

   "I have a person who I've been praying for; she could use some extra prayer. Would you pray for her too? She's really struggling."

   If the person asks for more details, just say:

   "The Lord knows who she is, and what she's struggling with; pray as He leads you. I wouldn't feel right divulging more details about her."

9. **DON'T BE OUTWARD FOCUSED:** Don't start with the outside in; rather start with the inside out. Too many mentors want to "help" someone change…by first changing how they dress, removing piercings, or altering how they talk. But Jesus warned against that: *You clean the outside of the cup and leave the inside dirty* (Luke 11:39). It's much more important to help a Girl with the inside stuff first—like her heart and spirit—because once that changes, the outside automatically begins to change.

10. **DON'T JUST TALK GOD:** Don't just talk about church and Jesus. Talk about other things too. Take her to places that aren't church related. Show her that Jesus can be included in all things. How about camping, the mall, dirt bike races, horseback riding, whale watching, a wedding, BBQ's, and the park?
11. **DON'T EXPECT THEY KNOW THE WORD:** Don't assume they "know" that scripture or Bible story. It bothers me when the pastor won't finish his thought.

"You all know the story of Esther, so I won't get into it," he says.

"No I don't, who is she?" And then, I'm lost.

12. **DON'T ASSUME SHE'S SAVED:** Even if she's a pastor's daughter, teaches a Bible study, or acts like a Christian, don't assume she's saved. I have led many Girls to the Lord who believed they were saved and weren't—and many who knew they *weren't* saved, but everyone else thought they were.
13. **DON'T EXPECT WHAT ISN'T THERE:** Don't expect her to act healthy if she isn't. The same goes for being saved. Don't expect an unsaved person to act saved.

How Jesus Mentored

- He approached them, no matter the cost of what others thought of Him
- He hung out with them
- Told them secrets
- Was obedient to His Father in front of them
- Did life alongside them
- Ministered and healed people in front of them

How Did Jesus's Disciples Respond?

- Followed Him
- Wanted to be with Him
- Hung out with Him

- Asked questions of Him,
- Obeyed Him
- Learned to trust Him
- Copied Him

Chapter 4—Tricks, Tactics, & Strategies

Drop Your Mask

How do you make a lifelong connection with someone? The easy—but not so easy to do answer—is drop your mask first. Learn to become a courageous person of integrity, by being the same on the inside and the out.

Share…Share…Share…Who are you? Where you do come from? How far has God brought you? Start sharing with women you feel comfortable with if you haven't done it yet. Get comfortable with your story and sharing it with others. Write it out if you haven't yet. We need to learn how to "drop our masks" on a regular basis. You never know who is listening.

1 Peter 3:15 says, *"Always be prepared to give an answer to everyone who asks you to give the reason for the hope that you have."* When was the last time you shared part of your story with someone—really shared? The only way to get comfortable sharing is to share and keep on sharing till it gets easier.

I first started sharing my story when I was in rehab one-on-one with women who were first getting there. I was the Queen of Masks, but I realized that if I dropped that mask for just a minute or two, I could relate to women and help them. I was drawn to the ones who wanted to leave. I would encourage them through my story by telling them that I wanted to do the same thing just weeks or months prior. I told them what helped me to stay. I was only a step or two ahead of them, and it comforted them to hear my story.

I was asked to share my story of physical abuse on a stage in front of a ton of people. It was for a black-tie affair celebrating the ten-year anniversary of an abuse recovery program I had gone through in rehab, and I had received a lot of healing from. It was so scary. I had to completely lean on the Lord to pull it off, but He gave me the words to say—and people were crying in the audience, and there was a whole lot of applause when I was done. When I shared that time, I noticed I still had my mask on; I didn't want them to know how bad it really was. I wasn't ready to admit that I was a victim, and I loved the attention I got afterwards. I definitely took some glory on that one.

I still speak on stages sharing my story, but my day-to-day sharing happens on Facebook as I share stories of my past through small snippets, combined with scripture. I blog parts of my story, but for the most part, I am always looking for ways to share my story even if it's very brief and just a small piece of it.

When I first meet people, I try to find ways to slip in that I'm a Christian; I tell them I come from a hard background or something about starting a ministry. I am trying to get them to engage and ask more questions. I'm also doing it because I'm looking for common ground where we can relate and instantly go deeper in relationship.

When was the last time you really shared part of your story with someone? The only way to get comfortable sharing is to share and keep on sharing till it gets easier. I share my story all the time now, but that was a long process for me. I used to call myself a chameleon, because I would change every time I was around new people. I became what I thought they would approve of, or I would shy away from sharing my story if I thought they would judge me, wouldn't be able to relate to me, or if I thought I needed to be more spiritually mature than I was at the time.

So when I first started learning about who I really was under all the masks, I would challenge myself to be my *real self* for as long as I could, as often as I could. I started out doing it for a few minutes at a time, until I got scared again and on the mask would go. Pretty soon, I was able to drop my mask for thirty minutes at a time and it increased from there.

I do feel that I've reached the place of no longer donning masks, but the only way I'm able to do that now is because I have learned to trust the Lord, not people, with my heart. So sharing intimate parts of my past—or current struggles—with strangers is not that difficult anymore, because I know that I am unconditionally loved by the Lord, and He does not judge me. *If God be for me, who can be against me?*

(Romans 8:31) Now don't get me wrong…I want people to like me. In fact, I still struggle with people-pleasing, however, I don't change who I am anymore to get that approval. If they don't approve of me, I will deal with it. I will not change who I am for anyone anymore. The vow I made to myself is "I will not take it up a notch or down a notch for anyone. I will be myself."

Depending on your position—whether it be mentor, minister, Bible study leader or the like—do yourself a favor. Don't put pressure on yourself to wear a mask with people, thinking you need to be at a "higher" level in your walk with the Lord than you are. When that temptation comes, and it will, resist it by remembering that Jesus chose you *just the way you are* to lead. He didn't wait until you were all cleaned up first. It's also important for those you mentor to know they can relate to you, because you are a real woman with real struggles too. A woman who serves God as a teacher, minister, or any other calling is absolutely dependent and surrendered to Him—but she is not perfect and she knows it; that's what keeps her humble. She knows whom she is in Him and that she needs Him to help her in everyday life.

There is a misconception about needing to be flawless, before you mentor. Newsflash: you don't have to be perfect! Nobody is.

Your story is your authority. Just like mine is. I mentor from my own experiences and through my relationship with the Lord. You don't need a terrible testimony either—it's okay to have had a wonderful childhood or healthy marriage. There is power in that story too. We can all relate to pain, disappointment, and tragedies. And we have all been forgiven of so much. Connect with yourself and your story, it has the ability of helping so many, if you would just be real with it. Get comfortable sharing your story and share it often. *We will overcome, by the blood of the Lamb and the word of our testimony*. (Revelation 12:11) So share it.

We only need to be a step or two ahead of another, before we can teach them something. For instance, remember the scripture that says *remove the log out of your own eye, SO THAT you can help remove the sliver out of another's eye* (Matthew 7:5)? Most of the mentoring I do comes from my own healing experience. I know what worked for me—and now that I know a lot of other women who have healed, I also know what worked for them. This enables me to give options, versus just one way. Healing is not a one-size-fits-all kind of thing.

I strongly suggest that you personally go through the 5 Steps (later described in Chapter 6) prior to taking others through it. Then you will have the experience, authority, and power from completing them. I don't like to tell anyone to do something that I haven't personally done myself. I think it's important to tell our Girls, "Look, I know this is going to be hard, because I did it too. However, it's worth it, and I'm right here with you while you complete it."

- When it comes to negative characteristics, Christian women are much less likely to admit to any of them.
- Women's Biggest Hurts: Christian women point to relationships as being the cause of their most significant heartache.
- We pressure ourselves as Christian women to behave in a certain way, to live up to an artificial ideal. If we can't measure up, we retreat, giving up the chance to have even one female friend with whom we can share our confidences without fear of reprise.

Finding the Root

She may have a drug issue or an eating disorder, she may cut herself or lead a promiscuous life, but that's not the issue—*those are the symptoms*. Through your talks and hanging out, be listening for the original CAUSE of the issues. Where did it all START? What happened to her that made her start to act out in that way? What is the ROOT? The root is an unresolved issue that is causing the symptom. Find the root, pull it out, and the symptom goes away.

Most issues like this are going to come from physical, sexual, mental, or emotional abuse, neglect, or abandonment—but not always. She could have been an only child with a mom who worked all

Website Citation: https://www.barna.org/culture-articles/587-christian-women-today-part-3-of-4-women-give-themselves-an-emotional-and-spiritual-check-up/#infographic

Website Citation: http://www.christianchronicle.org/article/its-time-to-be-transparent-women-need-close-christian-friendships the time; so she's used to getting her way. Whatever the case may be, the more you know about her, the more the evidence points to a certain root, or cause.

Most roots are attached to an unresolved issue that make them believe a lie that:

"I am not loved, or I am unworthy of love."

It's so crafty of the enemy to use that lie, because ***God is love*** and the greatest commandment is to love God and love people.

The root cause is generally an unresolved issue. It can be a lie, unhealed trauma, an unforgiven offense, unconfessed sin, a secret, etc. Asking questions will help you find it:

When do you remember first feeling like this?

Does this remind you of something in your past?

Or ask point-blank:

"What do you believe is the root cause of your current issue?"

The bigger the picture you have, the easier it will be to find the root, and in turn, help her remove it. Find the root and then rip it out. Ripping out the root is another term for resolving the unresolved issue. Hang on…you will learn how to do this in Chapter 6.

- Locate the root cause.
- Pull out the root.
- Symptoms go away.

SYMPTOMS

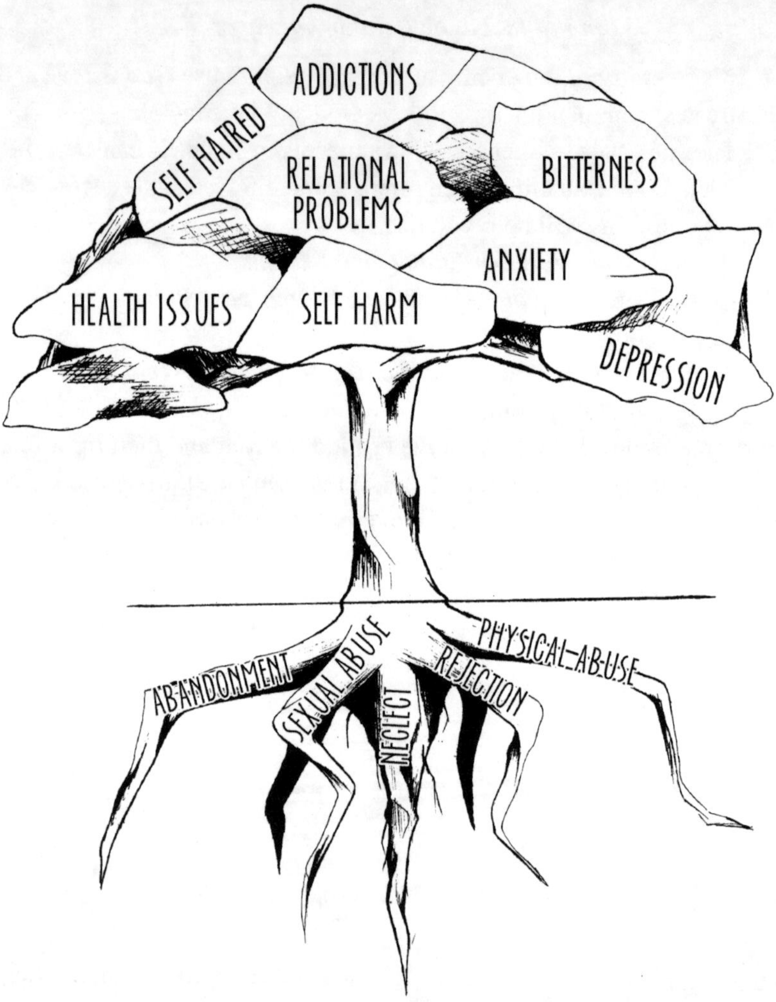

ROOT CAUSE

Understanding Triggers

You will hear this term used a lot, especially from people coming out of addictions or even counseling. Triggers remind us of something, or a situation, that makes us feel ashamed, and want to use drugs or alcohol, or return to old ways of unhealthy coping.

Satan uses triggers to keep us in bondage: *don't go there, don't eat that, don't smell that, don't listen to that....*

But God can use triggers to show us areas where He wants to heal us. The way I see triggers is the Lord putting His finger on a sore spot that reminds us of an unresolved issue. When that sore spot gets pushed, it points directly to the issue.

Once that unresolved issue is identified and then finally gets resolved—through confession, surrender, or forgiveness—then I highly suggest **replacing the old uncomfortable memory with a new memory**. It is a very powerful way to walk out your healing experience. For instance, the smell of vanilla coffee used to remind me of the first abortion I had when I was 19. I avoided that smell for many years, and once I forgave myself, I chose to make a new memory by drinking a cup with my husband and praying through the experience. Thus, replacing an old memory with a new memory. There is something tremendously healing when you do it.

Dangle the Carrot

I try to find out what she is called to do—or just really wants to do, but doesn't think she can. Whether she wants a spouse, ministry, or kids. I find what makes her tick and I paint a new dream for her by "dangling the carrot." This will help her do the hard work to heal as she keeps in mind the end goal (carrot). The strategy will reignite her hope, give her something to work for—by using her own words against her—and for you to slip God in...even if she doesn't recognize Him as God, YET.

Having a husband and ministry was the carrot that was dangled in front of me. I wanted a healthy husband, and I wanted to be a healthy wife, because I knew that unhealthy attracts unhealthy and I wanted nothing to do with that. I also desperately wanted to be used by God in service. Now I have both…a healthy husband and a ministry. I kept my eye on the prize (carrot).

My husband has said on numerous occasions, *"The hard work you put into healing not only benefits me and our marriage, but everyone your life touches. Thank you."*

Asking someone to heal for herself (who is spiritually and emotionally unhealthy) is an unreasonable request. Most Girls who come to you for help—especially in a desperate situation—have low self-worth and won't or can't do it for themselves. But they may do it for a future husband, career, or their future kids.

When I entered rehab in 2006, I hated myself; it was ridiculous to do it for *me*. I chose to get better for my boys. It wasn't until a year or so later, when I was able to do it for me too. People will often say "It won't work unless you do it for yourself." Well, I'm living proof that you don't have to start out that way. If I would have waited till I cared enough about myself to get the help I needed, I honestly don't think I would be alive right now.

Use Their Words Against Them

Do this in a nice, constructive way of course. "Remember, you said…?" The only way you can use this tactic is if you have *really been listening* to what they've been saying. You have to listen for what motivates her, or what she has noticed about herself. I had a Girl who was afraid to talk in public, even in small groups. I would say, "Okay, wait a minute—you're afraid to talk in front of this small group? Aren't you the Girl who rides those big huge horses?" Sometimes, you have to provoke them toward what they really want. What *they said* they wanted. Hold them true to their ow heart.

Open a Can

Tell it to her straight. Some women have never been told it straight. Some women have only heard, "It's not you. It's me." When you get to know her, you realize that it wasn't them, it's actually her. So love her enough to tell her the truth. *Know the truth and the truth will set you free* (John 8:32) even if the truth hurts a little, or a lot. There are ways to tell someone the truth in a loving, but straight-to-the-point way.

One time, there was a Girl who needed to be confronted. I was scared of her physically, so I prayed that the Lord would convict her heart—or have *someone else* confront her. He replied with, *"If you love her, **you'll** confront her."* Not the words I wanted to hear, but I still use them to this day—whenever I am afraid to confront someone by telling them a truth that is going to hurt them, and could possibly hurt our relationship. A huge part of mentoring is confronting issues in a person's life that are roadblocks to their growth. So…if you love her, you'll confront her.

Here's a piece of that story in her own words:

> "Michelle was the one person in my life who was willing to set fear aside, and face *me*—the real me. She called my bluff of masks I was donning, and continued(s) to tear down each one. I thought I knew my Savior, until Shell came toe to toe with me (literally), and stopped my quoting of all theological studies, and dared to challenge my heart.
>
> I vividly remember her battle cry, nose to nose with me, "I don't believe you have ever had a *relationship* with the ***real Jesus***." In total love, I wanted to tackle her, and pound her face in, proving that I knew the God of Love. But that was just it, I knew Abba, and studied thc Bible with Abba in my heart. But I feared Jesus, because I did not know the REAL JESUS. With the highest amount of patience and courage, Shell led me to the face of Jesus, to embrace a life of RELATIONSHIP with the Real Jesus, my Savior."
>
> ~ Billi Joy "Beej"

CHAPTER 5—DIRTY FILTERS

In a vehicle there are several filters that need to be replaced with clean filters in order for the vehicle to run at its optimum performance. That's the same way we as people are too. For instance, you're mentoring someone, and you say one thing—and she hears another. This is totally normal if they have a dirty filter. Keep in mind that I said "normal" not healthy. These are the situations where the patience and compassion of Christ have to kick in. It's annoying; I'm not going to lie.

You will try encouraging her to take a step in an area, and she will hear "You are not doing enough. You haven't healed at all." When you notice that she shuts down or gets mad, stop what you are doing and ask, "What just happened? Did I say something to offend or hurt your feelings?" And then explain what you meant to communicate, mixed with encouragement. If she chooses to remain stubborn...repeat yourself, and then let her know you love her and when she is ready to talk about it, she can call you. It is not about you—this is about her and the hurtful lies she's still packing around.

Sometimes, just confessing the lie that is making the filter dirty—and having someone challenge it—can bring healing. It is the truth that sets us free.

Is there an area of your life where you know you have a *dirty filter*? For instance, if anyone said or questioned ANYTHING about my parenting, I heard, "You're a bad mom."

Common Lies Women Believe (that can make the filter dirty)

- It's too late for me, I'm not a virgin anymore
- I've crossed the line of no return
- I was born this way

- Beauty is a curse
- How could a guy like him fall for a girl like me?
- I'm dirty
- God could never use me; I'm too far gone
- Everybody leaves me
- Nothing ever lasts

Common Lies Men Believe (that can make the filter dirty)

- I will fail if I try
- I don't measure up
- He is better than me
- I don't have what it takes
- I can't win
- No one will know
- I can't be honest about that
- I'm the only one who has ever struggled with this
- I can't recover from that
- I can't be the spiritual leader of my home

Lies, Labels, & Thoughts

A lot of Girls that you will end up mentoring have let their thoughts run rampant and have free reign. They have to be taught how to take their thoughts captive. They have to learn how to make new habits to replace the unhealthy habits by CHOOSING to think on things that are positive, truthful and helpful.

You can't control the thoughts that pop up in your head, but you can control how long you think about them.

Take every thought captive (2 Corinthians 10:5). How in the world do you do that? The word *take* is an action word—you have to *do* something! God never tells us to do something that He hasn't given us the ability to pull off. If He says we can do it, then we can.

When an inappropriate thought comes in, I immediately distract my attention and pray, "Lord help me." Then I will sing a song like

"Jesus, Lover of My Soul." I refuse to allow my brain to just think about whatever it wants to. I will glorify the Lord in my body and my mind.

Thoughts become actions and so do lies and labels. People believe certain lies about themselves that can turn into labels, such as "Bad Parent," "Stupid" or "Slut." People have made bad choices, but that shouldn't define who they are. Bad choices and sins do not make up a person's identity, however they will view those labels and lies as truth. It's our job to show them that they are not true.

First Impressions

When you first start mentoring someone, keep in mind, her body language may say something totally different than her thoughts.
She may look like she is thinking…

"I don't like you, and I don't care what you or anyone else thinks."
But really, she is thinking…
"Please don't leave me."
"HELP ME."
"I'm not like you…you were born good, but I was born bad."
"You don't understand."
"If you really knew me, you wouldn't love me."
"I wish I had a life like yours."
"I wish I was sure about God like you are."
"I don't want to be a burden to you."
"You will leave me like everyone else has."

What They're Thinking

When you tell her that you need to talk to her, she's thinking:

"You're mad at me."
"What did I do wrong?"

A good way to handle this ahead of time, is to say:

"Don't worry, you're not in trouble. I'm not mad at you."

What They Need to Hear from You

"I won't leave you or give up on you. You will have to leave me."

"I love you, and I believe in you."

"If I can do it, anyone can."

"I'm so sorry for what you've gone through. It's over now. You don't need to survive through it. You have survived."

"You're not alone anymore. We're here for you."

"The Lord loves you so much. He thinks you're awesome, and so do I."

Chapter 6—The 5 Steps of Purely His

- Preparing for the Steps
- What to Look For
- How Long
- Don't Skip Steps

Preparing for the Steps

The intention of these steps is to help people go ALL-IN with Jesus while getting UNSTUCK from anything in the way of that. Once a person goes *all-in*, everything else begins to fall into place. We should give them hope and encourage them toward a better life—their best life. It can be accomplished through a relationship with you and others. Jesus was, and is, very relational. His style worked, so we would be wise to mimic His example.

These steps are an outline as you are mentoring. Don't take a cheesy approach and tell people what step you are on. Keep it in the back of your mind. It's the direction you're taking them, and the steps to take them there.

The questions and the other tools are provided to get to the heart of the matter and build real relationships for all those you're mentoring, including yourself. It's an opportunity to facilitate a Sisterhood (Band of Brothers) that will last a lifetime, so no one needs to feel alone anymore. Mentors need to lead by example; so you go first. Knowing answers to the questions will help you dialoge when asking someone else. Don't try to be perfect or more spiritual than you really are. Being imperfect gives those you minister to an opportunity to minister to you as well.

You can say, "Well, this is how I answered that question" or "Let me tell you a little about me." Get comfortable with your story and sharing it with others. Write it out if you haven't yet. We need to practice "dropping our masks" on a regular basis.

They triumphed over him by the blood of the Lamb and by the word of their testimony; they did not love their lives so much as to shrink from death.
— Revelation 12:11

Most people enjoy engaging in deep conversation. Now, I know that there are exceptions—especially in front of people—but generally, individuals want to be known and to know others. It is usually a matter of trusting that will help them share more. As they share their stories out loud, they will discover things about themselves that they didn't realize—and they could even be healed on the spot, because they will speak out truth about themselves and finally believe them. They will also speak out lies and you will be able to point them out.

When I mentioned that we were starting support groups for men, I heard a lot of people say, "Good luck with that. Men don't like to talk like women do." We, as a society, tend to stereotype men.

My answer to that is "You're right. They don't talk like women—they talk like men." There are plenty of men who enjoy talking. When a man decides that he's ready to go all-in and wants to get unstuck from things in the way of that, then nothing stops him. Our groups run for two hours each week, and there is *no dead time* in the men's group or the women's group.

People automatically connect to each other when they find common ground in their stories—and there is *always* common ground. Try to get them to engage and ask more questions. Look for the common ground where you can relate, and instantly go deeper in relationship. No one connects on superficial topics—**we need to go deeper, and that takes our trusting in the Lord, not the other person's response to our story.**

What to Look For

It is important to learn to listen to her and the Lord at the same time. Learn to discern what she is really trying to say. Shut your mouth long enough to listen and be praying in your head, *"God give me wisdom. What's going on here?"*

There is a time to listen, and a time to shut it, a time to hug, and a time to just let her sit in the mess she has created. Don't rush in with the hug; let the tears happen. Tears are good—they are healing. Good listeners also ask a lot of questions to clarify and make it easier for her to go deeper. It helps her know that you really care too. When you take the time to listen and ask more questions, it communicates that she is valued and worth your time. Don't rush to give her the answer or fix the problem.

The following questions are designed to go deeper. When a Girl answers them, she will discover things about herself that she wasn't aware were issues. It will also help her get prepared to be mentored and be a part of a group atmosphere that is designed to be transparent. It will help you get a big picture of who she is REALLY and what her beliefs are.

Asking these questions begins when you first start talking to her, but that doesn't mean you are done with this step, you will always refer back to it and go deeper later. The first step is about laying the foundation. It is also very important that she hears your answers too; this is how you will bond on a deeper level, which lasts a lifetime. Relationships are built through connecting on a deep level, which comes from finding common ground in our stories, and thus building trust and friendships.

How Long?

These steps are most effectively used over a five-month period through one of our Purely His Mentoring Groups (see chapter 8). However, these steps can be used by anyone who is leading a group or mentoring one on one, including parents.

Over a two-hour coffee date with a Girl, I went through a version of every step, and by the time we were done, she had made the choice to go all-in with Jesus and she got unstuck in some areas of her life. Keep in mind—my mentoring style is bold and straight to the point. I don't waste a lot of time when I see where they are stuck.

Your mentoring style will be different than mine, and that's okay. The Lord made us all different, and this system can work with all personalities. A lot of it depends on the person you are mentoring, and their willingness to *go for it* or linger in the pain of their past.

Don't Skip Steps

You will find that most people will want to skip steps—especially if there are addictions in their past. She will want everything NOW. Encourage her to take her time in healing; don't skip any steps, just to "get it done." You want complete healing, lacking nothing, not partial-healing that needs to be revisited all the time, because it wasn't done right the first time. Now, this doesn't mean it has to take a really long time either, it just means do a thorough job while persevering.

With our 5-step process, they are designed to go in order, but they can be repeated over and over again, and then done out of sequence once they've been gone through once. You may find that someone is not ready to fully go through and look at their relationship with the Lord yet, so you may just skim over that step the first time, and decide to come back later. It's important to meet people where they truly are.

Some people will want to jump straight to Step Five: *Take Someone with You*, but they need to take care of themselves first—before trying to help another—so that they can be better equipped to help them.

Another thing to remember is that we are not 100% responsible for a person's growth and healing. We may only get through one or two steps with a person, but then another person comes around and takes them through step three. It is a huge blessing to take someone through all five steps, but as long as they get there—who really cares who helped them? Besides, we need to always remember that it is God who actually does the healing and makes a person grow. We're stronger together than we are apart—we're a good team.

I planted the seed in your hearts, and Apollos watered it, but it was God who made it grow.

— 1 Corinthians 3:6 (NLT)

When I'm working with a Girl, I only deal with what is on top—with what is bothering her the most—then I find the root cause of that issue and help her rip it out. Some issues are deeper, and shouldn't have a time limit…however…I don't think we should take our sweet time with it either. We are all a work in progress, and we will not be complete until the day we step into Heaven. So take a deep breath, and remove the pressure of healing completely *right away*. The Lord has a huge heart for freedom, and wants us free more than we do! Be encouraged that He is heal you and set you free, and won't stop until He's done.

…he who began a good work in you will carry it on to completion until the day of Christ Jesus.

— Philippians 1:6

Here is the 5-Step Process I use as an outline when I'm mentoring. It gives a framework and direction to what you're already doing. The steps build on each other, and should be used *in order* the first time around with someone. After that, you will repeat part of the steps at times and you'll be able to recognize where someone is in the sequence of steps, and then focus on one of the steps more than another.

You'll find that these steps are dynamic—and can be custom designed for your style of mentoring, and the particular people you're working with. Sometimes, you will use several steps all at once, and go back through it many times. But the MAIN THING stays the MAIN THING, which is to help them choose to go *all-in* with Jesus, and *get unstuck* from anything that's holding them back. These steps offer an outline, as well as a desired purpose and how to get the Girls there… versus just being a Christian buddy who happens to be a good listener.

It Works

This method can work for anyone—no matter what her background or current situation is. Don't focus on the *symptom* such as self-harm, eating disorder, drug addiction, or promiscuity, etc. But rather focus on the *root*. Every Girl has a dream—or had one, and she has probably just lost hope in it. That's what makes this step universal.

STEP ONE: *Your Story*
STEP TWO: *HIS Story*
STEP THREE: *Get Unstuck*
STEP FOUR: *Walk it Out*
STEP FIVE: *Take Someone with You*

STEP ONE: *Your Story*

I praise you because I am fearfully and wonderfully made;
your works are wonderful, I know that full well.

— Psalm 139:14

Description:

Don't take it up a notch or down a notch for anyone. A woman of integrity is the same wherever she goes—her insides match her outsides. She doesn't don a bunch of hats, masks, or costumes. Learn to be cool with your strengths and weaknesses. Realize and accept the real you. Learn to love yourself—then, you can get the focus off you, and put it on others.

This will create a newfound confidence where you can just settle into being yourself; your Girls will follow.

Learning, and then living out our true identities in Christ is foundational to our healthy walks with Him. Many well-meaning mentors, however, start pouring in teachings about identity in Christ without meeting the Girl where she truly is, thus skipping a necessary step. When we go about it in this manner, we teach them how to *fake it*. They will begin *acting* like a Christian before they believe it or feel like one. It's important to help them build a solid foundation, so that they will be able to stand the test of time and never go backward.

I can't tell you how many people have said to me:

"I don't know who I am. I've lost myself."

I can personally relate to those statements. When I had come out of my last abusive relationship, I said:

"If you were to ask me who I am or what I really like to do,

I honestly couldn't answer you.

I feel like I'm upside down and inside out.

I don't know who I am anymore."

Now, I realize that every person is in a different place spiritually and emotionally, so maybe they aren't lost completely, but just a little misplaced.

Relationship is key when using these steps; they won't be effective if you don't develop a relationship. Regardless of where that Girl is in her life, God has made your paths cross; so get to know her, and allow her to get to know you too—then, see what happens. It's important to start with sharing your stories.

"Nobody cares how much you know, until they know how much you care."

—Theodore Roosevelt

Set the expectation for the ones you're mentoring by being deeper and more authentic. This is a step of love in action. She should share, *and so should you*. No questions should be off limits concerning your story. Before you try to change her behavior, get to know her heart. This is how you build real relationships. You will connect on a deep level by "dropping your mask and keeping it real."

Knowing who we are in Christ is absolutely foundational, but you can't get her there until you know what she believes about herself. You have to meet her *there* first. When a Girl has "lost" herself, it's our job to listen to the whole story and find her. Some people's greatest quest is to find their identity. When a Girl knows who she is—then she will tend to stop striving and desperately looking for validation. We want her to get to the point where she accepts and even embraces her strengths and weaknesses. God made us all with weaknesses and strengths, which is the reason we need each other. He wants us to depend on one another.

Some might ask, "What's the point in having someone share their story?" My answer to that is *because they will learn to trust again*, and see that others struggle in the same way. They will make real and lifelong connections. It also relieves some of the pressure from family and friends, because they can spread their eggs around to different baskets instead of having all of them in one. This brings things that were once in the dark out into the light, which makes the lies lose their power. Confession is a huge part of healing, and it takes place very naturally in this context. We know that we overcome the enemy by the blood of the Lamb and the word of our testimony (Revelation 12:11).

Talking openly with someone and asking all types of questions will help create lifelong bonds. It will help them discover and reconnect to themself, the Lord, and others. People need to be heard, known, and loved for *who they are right now*, and *for the real person under all the junk*, not just for who they WILL be.

How will she be different after going through this step? A person becomes unstoppable when she is truly confident in who she is. She will stop searching, and start living. She will be comfortable in her own skin, and start taking risks again. She will usually start making healthy choices to reflect her newly-discovered identity.

A woman who knows who she is—and accepts herself—has a humble confidence that gives her what she needs to conquer anything…including a failing marriage, strained relationships, going back to college, and improving her work performance (to name a few).

Making a solid relationship with her will give you permission to mentor her.

The Big Picture

One of the best ways to start this process is by *asking a lot of questions* when you first meet her. This will allow you to see the **big picture** of whom she believes she is, and be able—at the right time—to show her what her true identity is.

The goal of this step is to uncover her real identity, and help her feel confident in her God-given unique identity. She needs to know that she matters—by you asking deep questions, investing the time, and sharing your story with her—she will begin to feel that.

If you pay close attention, you will see the real person under all the junk; you will discover that God created her. What He creates, lasts—no matter how many bad choices she's made, or traumas she's experienced. What I have found through my own life, and the lives of others, is that the real person is just covered up by a bunch of junk, but she's still in there. People always want to add to themselves, but I say, "Get rid of stuff; don't add anymore. What God created was fearfully and wonderfully made, and we can't improve on that."

Through this process, you will be able to identify:

- The areas where she is stuck, because of unresolved issues.
- How the Lord could use hard things in her past to help others if she gets healthy.
- Her God-given calling in life.
- Her motivation for getting mentored or wanting to be healed, which can be used as the "carrot" to dangle in front of her to encourage growth.
- Learn the lies she believes about herself, which have become labels.

Watch and intently listen for her labels, addictions, struggles, points of un-forgiveness, poor self-image, and lies. These are all symptoms of a deeper issue, or root. There are usually one or two. Try not to pay attention so much to the *symptoms*, but rather *what caused them*. In "Step Three: Get Unstuck," we will discuss how to pull the roots out.

As the mentor, it's important for you to try and figure out where your mentee is at spiritually and emotionally. How does she REALLY feel about herself, and what does she REALLY think about God? The more you know about her, the easier you can lead her. Remember that the Lord is ALL about relationships with Him and others, and He values LOVE more than anything.

Ask the Lord for wisdom on what each Girl is called to do for Him. Watch what makes her cry or really excites her, when it comes to helping others, because these emotions are potentially pointing to her God-given calling.

Watch to see what still makes her angry, or guilty from past experiences—it could be something she needs to be free from.

Don't just listen to someone's words…watch to see if her body language matches. Watch where there is a lot of emotion, but she says, "I've let that go, though." *Wrong*. She *thinks* she "let it go," but her face tells you differently.

Pray in your mind while she's talking, "Lord, show me what you want me to see. Give me wisdom."

- Pay attention when someone keeps repeating the same story. That is a classic indicator that she is stuck there.
- Begin connecting the dots, "Oh, that's why she's like that…that's why she reacts that way."

Questions to get the big picture. Pick and choose what to ask, or come up with your own set of questions. I believe you should answer these questions alone, with a friend, or a mentor of yours. You will find out so much about yourself. I have found that the Lord reveals things to me as I write or share with others.

Here are some common questions I ask to get to the heart of the matter, and build a relationship:

- Who are you?
    - Tell me about yourself.
- What was your relationship like with your parents as you were growing up?
    - How did your dad interact with you?
    - How did your mom interact with you?
    - What is your relationship like with them now?
- Who were you as a little kid?
    - What did you like to wear or play?
    - What did you dream of being when you grew up?

- If you could help any type of person—anywhere in the world—who would it be?
    - What makes you cry?
    - What really has your heart?
- If you could do absolutely anything in the world, and get paid for it…what would it be?
- Who were you before all the trauma of life?
    - What traumas or hard times have you experienced?
- What has been your greatest disappointment so far?
- What has been your greatest joy so far?
- What are your strengths and weaknesses?
- What do you believe others think of you?
    - The negative and positive?
- What is something about you that others wouldn't normally guess?
- What is your negative self-talk?

All these questions are being asked so that you can see the big picture, which will help you see how God could, or has, *worked all things together for good* (Romans 8:28), which can encourage her that it wasn't all done in vain. Plus, you can see her purpose, and what she loves. ***Sometimes, our greatest hurts and darkest sins become our stage for ministry after we get the victory.***

Asking these questions will help create lifelong bonds additionally, they will help her discover and reconnect to herself and to the Lord. She needs to be heard, known, and loved for who she is right now—for the real and current person she is, not just whom she will be. If you really listen, you will see where she is stuck.

This step is designed for you to discover where she's REALLY at, and for you to know what you're working with. This step is laying the foundation. It is also very important that she hears *your* answers too, because that is how you will both bond on a deeper level that will last a lifetime.

Real Life Example

I was working with this Girl who came from a hard past, which included divorce, witchcraft, alcoholism, physical abuse, heroin addiction, and foster care—just to name a few. I had such a heart for her, and wanted to help her immediately. I knew I had to "play my cards right," because her wall was high and thick. I knew a little bit about her story, so I was able to share certain parts of my story that I knew she could relate to. My initial purpose was to find common ground with her, in order to start a relationship. I wanted her to see that I could understand where she was at, and I wasn't judging her. I was hoping that our initial meeting would give her hope.

Here is an example of what a real conversation with a Girl going through "Step One: *Your Story*" might look like.

> **Me:** Wow, thanks for sharing your story with me. I know things have been rough, and you're having a hard time seeing any good that could come out of this, but I want you to know that we all blow it. Some people choose never to come up out of that, and some do. I chose to start living a new life, and now I've been healthy for several years now. I've never backslidden. I'm totally doing what I love, which is mentoring others through, and out of, hard and what seems like hopeless situations. So if I can do it, anyone can—*including you*. First off, you are 19 and trying to get help. I was 30 before I finally asked for help; so you're already eleven years ahead of me. Just imagine where you'll be at 30?
>
> **Girl:** Yah, but you're different than me. I've been like this all my life!
>
> **Me:** Really…all your life? Because when you were sharing your story, ***you said*** that you were a hopeful, trusting, and excited little girl, but after you experienced that trauma, it all changed for you. So can you see that your identity changed at that age? You were born with a God-given unique personality and dreams. But along the way, your true identity has been covered up by other people's poor choices, and now your own too. But the REAL you is still in there.

Girl: Yes, I remember being like that, and I wish I was still like that, but it would be stupid to be so trusting in this world with the way things are.

Me: True. I totally get that. Life has taught you not to trust, so why in the world would you? Speaking of trust, I want to thank you for the trust you've given me today by sharing such hard details about your life. I will do my best to hold your heart carefully, so that you can begin to trust again. But even with me—it's best for you to trust *the Lord* with your heart, and not me, because He will never fail you, but I will, not intentionally, but it's likely because I'm human.

Girl: I just feel so weighted down with all this stuff…I don't know if I will ever be healthy like you. You are so confident and happy. I'm the complete opposite.

Me: Well…sweetie, I wasn't always confident and happy. I had to commit to allowing the Lord to heal those areas of my life that were weighing me down. I chose to listen to what the Lord and other healthy people said about who I *really was* until I could believe it myself. I still have women who speak truth over me and encourage me when I'm down. We need each other for that.

Girl: I want to be like you someday. I hate myself.

Me: I don't hate you. I think you're pretty cool actually, and you should stay yourself, because too many of me running around would make this place annoying. God likes diversity, and so do we, really. When you were sharing about your life dreams and desires, ***you said*** that you always dreamed of being a child psychologist. This shows me that you have a heart to help those who can't help themselves—a voice for those who have lost theirs, and you want kids to experience healing. I think that's amazing.

Girl: Yes, I DID want to be a child psychologist, but that's not possible now. No one will want to hire someone with the things I've done. I let that dream die a long time ago.

Me: When I was in rehab, a friend of mine sent me a letter with a hot pink post-it note stuck to it that read: IT'S NEVER

TOO LATE TO BE WHAT YOU MIGHT HAVE BEEN. I instantly thought, "I always wanted to be a counselor." Well…I might not have a degree or anything, but through my life experiences, I am able to counsel a lot of women and girls. I didn't learn this stuff from a book other than the Bible, but I learned through my own experience of healing.

I can totally see you becoming a child psychologist when you get all healed up. In fact, it's a great motivator not to skip any steps. Think back to when you were having issues and your parents, or the foster system, sent you to see a counselor or psychologist. Couldn't you tell the ones who didn't know what they were talking about, and couldn't relate to you at all? Most of them, right? What if you decided *right now* to go for it? Not to skip any steps…so that you can speak with authority ***when*** you tell your little clients to do something that you have actually done yourself.

Girl: You said you can TOTALLY see me as a child psychologist? Even though I have a black eye right now, just put down the bottle, and you just heard my story? How can *someone like me* become something like that?

Me: The simple answer is God. *With God, ALL things are possible* (Matthew 19:26). Look at me. I was a meth addict, and now I'm the women's minister of a Christian ranch. I know you don't believe in Him at this point, and that's fine. Here's another thing to think about: you can relate to so many different types of people because of what you've gone through…abandonment, abuse, addiction, witchcraft, suicide attempts, overdoses, divorce…I mean really, who *can't* you connect with? I believe that you will be a great asset to someone when you get to a healthy place.

Practical Tools

I like to give my Girls "Identity in Christ" scriptures list and ask them to circle the ones they don't believe. Through this, I can further see where they are stuck. (These tools are provided in a Sisterhood or Band of Brother's Box-see Chapter 8)

You can also ask them to write on an index card three words to describe themselves and three words to describe God. Hold onto it for a few months, then ask them to do the same thing and watch how different their answers are. Show them both cards side by side, because most people will not feel like they've changed—when in reality, they have changed a lot.

Encourage them to read their Bible and attend church, because it is the Word of God that will truly change them.

Have them journal who they really are, and who they really dream of being.

Other Thoughts on Your Story

God has given each of us a unique personality *and it is not something to repent from*. Yes, you need to get rid of sin, but not your personality. If you're a fighter, loud, strong-willed, sensitive and emotional… God made you unique and He will use the REAL YOU. An effective mentoring relationship should provide an environment where a person is validated for their REAL identity.

A startling 42% say faith communities do not offer them any emotional or social support "at all.

One-third (34%) admits to not receiving much or any support from their church.

Website Citation: https://www.barna.org/barna-update/culture/649-three-major-faith-and-culture-trends-for-2014#.U2VPc_ldWQw

Desired Outcome

Each one of these steps stands alone, but they work most effectively when all 5 Steps are completed in sequence. When the Girl from the former example completed this step, she had her hope reignited, which is absolutely necessary for healing to take place. *Hope differed makes the heart sick* (Proverbs 13:12). And believe me, her heart was sick; I could tell by looking at her. As we talked, I saw hope ignite in her eyes, especially when I mentioned that it wasn't too late for her to become a child psychologist. I call that glimmer in her eye *The Carrot*. She also felt heard, understood, and accepted, which translates into love—and *love covers a multitude of sins* (1 Peter 4:8). The other part that took place was a confession of her sins, which as soon as a Girl does it, lightens the load.

I also explained to her there was just a bunch of junk covering the *real her*, and told her I would help her get rid of it. This set her up for what was going to be coming around the corner…the next steps.

How will your Girl act, think, or feel after this step? She will feel heard, seen, and appreciated. This will give her hope. She will also feel connected to you emotionally because both of you shared your stories.

STEP TWO: *HIS Story*

"But who do you say that I am?"
…"You are the Christ, the Son of the living God."

— Matthew 16:15-16

Description

This section is ***huge***! **Don't assume she is saved**, even if her dad was a pastor, she sang on the worship team, or she knows the Bible like a theologian. Being saved is more than just being a good person or knowing stuff about God. *It's a relationship with Jesus*. The Lord wants all of you, not just a part of you. He wants to be your first love, not your last. He wants you to stop living for yourself, and everyone else, and start living for Him.

If you truly want to love the Lord and learn to live for Him, then make the gut-wrenching choice to do whatever it takes to put Him first. I promise you—it will be the best choice you ever, ever make. He will make your life fall into place. He will change your life, and give it purpose. He will fill you in ways you have always desired, but felt out of reach. He will give you the strength and power to stop doing things you shouldn't, and equip you to do the things you should *and* were created for. You are all literally one choice away from a complete life change.

The goal of this step is to find out where your Girl is really at with the Lord, and then help her realize who He really is—and help her make the choice to give her life to Him. It's important to be very delicate with this step. This is a crucial step, which affects *everything*. This is not the time to push—that will come later on, when the relationship is on more solid ground. This is a step of *listening* more than anything, because you are still building a strong foundation of trust.

It doesn't matter where this Girl comes from, or how deep her hurt or hate is. This step is necessary with everyone. If you listen closely, you will hear where she is stuck. You will hear what she believes about God, and how it is different than the God you know (the real God of the Bible). Most Girls I've worked with are mad at God on some level—even self-professed atheists. No one ever seems to blame Satan. Commonly, I hear, "God is the only one who could have stopped it, but He didn't. He allowed it to happen."

The Heart of the Matter

Who do you say I am? It's important to start with *who she really believes He is*, not what she *should say*. A lot of people know the "right" answers, but they don't really believe them based on their life experiences. Here are some questions that can help you get to the heart of the matter. I don't suggest asking these questions in order, just choose the ones that fit into the conversation you're already having. Act naturally.

- Who is God?
  - What does God look like to you?
  - What is His personality, character, facial expression?
- When did you meet Him?
  - Tell us about the day you got saved.
- What does He think of you?
  - What do you think of Him?
- What do you have against Him?
  - What does He have against you?
- What do you wish your relationship looked like with Him?
  - Why can't you have that?
  - What's in the way?
- Is there someone who has a relationship with Him that you envy? Why?
- Do you have a different relationship with God, Jesus, and the Holy Spirit? Or is it the same?
- Did your relationship look different before all of your own sin?
  - When did it change?
- Have you ever given your whole life to Him?
  - What part are you still holding back?
- Tell me about a time when you heard God, felt Him, and knew it was Him?
  - How does He generally talk to you?

Website Citation: http://www.focusonthefamily.com/faith/becoming_a_christian/how_do_i_find_the_right_church/overcoming_a_bad_church_experience.aspx?p=1

You don't have to join a cult to have a bad church experience. Approximately 22 million Americans say they are Christians and made a faith commitment to Jesus Christ, and say that commitment is still important to them, but they have struggled with faith or relational issues and therefore quit going to church. Tens of thousands more will join their ranks this week. Like a safe harbor, local churches can be a second home for many people. Sadly, churches also can be the setting for some of the harshest attacks against our faith.

Those who avoid Christian churches, one of the driving forces behind such behavior is the painful experiences endured within the local church context. In fact, one Barna study among unchurched adults shows that nearly four out of every ten non-churchgoing Americans (37%) said they avoid churches because of negative past experiences in churches or with church people.

Real Life Example

I met a lady while my husband and I were doing business with her. He had been a customer there for many years, but I was new to her. She went into a little bit of her story, and just by listening, I was able to identify an area where she was stuck.

I had only met her twice at that point, so it was a little awkward, but I finished a few of her sentences—she quickly realized that I knew what I was talking about. I invited her to have coffee with me sometime soon. She looked surprised and interested, but definitely hesitant. My husband perked up, and began vouching for me and my competency in this area. She looked at him and looked back at me several times. A week later, I got a text, and we set up a coffee date.

She's in her 40s, married to her second husband, has one grown daughter, professes Christianity, doesn't attend church, is a heavy drinker, and struggles with anxiety. She had been a teller at a bank when the place was robbed several years prior, and that's when everything changed.

We spent about two hours together in a corner of a coffee shop. She told me *Her Story*, and I told her parts of mine that she could relate to. When the walls were down and I knew she trusted me—and I had enough information to see what the problem was— I stepped into this step and this is what it looked like.

Girl: So what do you think I should do? Is there hope for me?

Me: Absolutely, there's hope for you. I know life seems pretty hard right now, and it's been messed up ever since the robbery happened. What I realized as you were talking, is that your control was taken from you that day—so now, you live your life controlling everything, so that you won't ever be taken by surprise again. The other thing I noticed is that you felt abandoned by God in that moment, and you are mad at Him for not protecting you. So you have decided not to develop a relationship with him anymore—because you don't trust Him, and you definitely don't want Him in control, because He let that burglary happen. Am I correct?

The tears began to flow. That is a clear sign to me that I just hit the target, and the Lord was speaking through me.

Girl: Yes! I want to trust Him, but I don't understand why he let that happen to me? I have been shaken up ever since that day. I don't even know where my Bible or Christian CDs are anymore. I left everything that day, because I felt like He deserted me; I didn't understand, because I was a good person. I decided that day that I would never allow anyone to be in control of me again—including Him.

Me: I have a little different picture when I look at the same situation, but that's easy when it didn't happen to me. God loves us enough—and He loves us so much—that He doesn't control our choices; He blessed us with free will. There are definitely those times and those people that we wish we could take away their free will, but we can't. When I look at that day, I see that God *did* protect you, because here I am sitting across from you, and you're alive. You also weren't wounded physically that day, AND the guy got caught. He's still in prison for the crime. So, although the Lord allowed the man to make his own choice to commit that crime, He also protected you from something happening even worse to you. He was there when it happened, and He's still here with you.

Girl: I guess that's true; I never thought of what *could have happened*, or what He saved me from. I just couldn't understand why it happened to me.

Me: In hard times, some people cling to the Lord, and some get as far away from Him as possible.

Girl: Yah, that's what I did. I felt like I could only trust myself, but now I'm finding that I can't even trust myself—because now I'm drinking every night and I'm not happy. I'm so mad at God though. I totally feel like He has sent me to the corner because I'm in trouble and is waiting until I get my act together again.

Me: He didn't put you in that corner. You did. The enemy put you in a prison of fear, resentment, and independence. The Lord wants to tell you that *He came to set the captive free* (Luke 4:18). He has opened the doors to the prison you're in, and says, "Come out—you're free." He's not mad at you. He was there that day. He knows why you've been feeling and acting this way. He just misses you, and wants to hang out with you again.

Girl: So He's not mad at me?

Me: Nope. He loves you, and misses you. He's saying, "Sweetie, I know you're scared, and I understand why, but come out of that corner, and LIVE. *My perfect love will cast out all that fear* (1 John 4:18).

Girl: I feel so bad that I left Him too; I didn't know what else to do. I can't believe I got tricked into thinking He was mad at me.

Me: Are you ready to come out of that prison and go all-in with Jesus again?

Girl: I totally am. I'm so sick of feeling this way. I'm starting not to even recognize myself anymore, because I've gotten so scared, so bitter, and I'm normally a very happy-go-lucky kinda Girl. It's time.

These steps naturally flow together but you will primarily pull from *Your Story* as a foundation, because you will remind them of who they actually are.

What Was I Thinking?

Notice how I was able to give her the picture I could see? It's easy to do when you are not personally involved in the emotions of what happened. Anyone can do it. Just make sure you *validate* how you would probably feel the same way, but because you're on the outside looking in, you have a different perspective.

She was stuck in fear and resentment. I ended up walking her through forgiving God for not protecting her. Even if He did protect her from dying, she felt He hadn't protected her from the robbery itself—so her perception was her reality. I helped her remember who she was, and how this event had changed her. I helped her miss her old self.

She had hope, was relieved, and encouraged. I sent her away with *homework* per se. I encouraged her to begin *acknowledging Him in all her ways* (Proverbs 3:6) and start including Him in her daily life.

No matter what you're doing, begin talking to the Lord to remind yourself that He really is there. If you are a Christian, then He goes everywhere you go: the bathroom, car, doing the dishes, church, the park—wherever you go, He goes. So quit ignoring Him, and talk to Him; include Him in everything. He's there to ask advice from, thank Him for things, comfort you, provide whatever you need, teach you, direct you, convict you of wrong doing, and give you the words to help another. He is the Great I AM, able to be anything you need and want Him to be. He is Emmanuel–*God with us*.

Estranged from God

His Story is in the Bible, so get to know Him all over again. Read it relationally, not religiously. Too many Christians read the Bible because they HAVE to, and they lose their passion for the Lord. Instead, begin reading scripture as a conversation with the Lord. Ask Him questions as you go, relating to Him in the process. You're already good, because of what Jesus did for you, so start enjoying your walk with Him.

If you want to become Christ-like, then hang out with Christ, and the people that represent Him well. We are a reflection and the most similar to the five people we hang out with the most. Know Him—know you—because all the answers we're looking for are in Him. *Seek first His kingdom and His righteousness, and all these things will be given to you as well* (Matthew 6:33).

In all your ways acknowledge Him, and He shall direct your paths (Proverbs 3:6, KJV). This is the scripture I use to remind myself how to include Him in my daily life. For instance: I will be driving somewhere "by myself" and out loud I'll say, *"So Lord, what should we do today?"* or *"I'm so glad you're with me right now, and I'm not alone."*

The other thing that is common for me to do is talk to Him on a regular basis all day long. I say the word *Lord* so much I have called my husband and my son "Lord" before. *Acknowledging Him* is just choosing not to ignore Him anymore. He's right there all the time; it's rude to ignore Him. So knock it off, and watch your life change!

His Story is in the Bible. Get to know Him all over again. Read your Bible relationally, not religiously.

Listen Well

Really listen to her answers about ***knowing Him***. I have led quite a few Girls to the Lord who no one would have guessed were not saved—including herself. The majority are saved, maybe backslidden, but saved. However, they have never given their WHOLE life to Jesus, and that is a simple process of her making the choice to go *all-in*. That happens with her making the decision, and then follow it up with a prayer just to "seal the deal."

Encourage her just to talk to God just like she's talking to you. Help her learn to hear the voice of the Lord. The most important thing we can do for her is to show her how to have a relationship with Him. *Seek first his kingdom and his righteousness, and all these things will be given to you as well* (Matthew 6:33). When she puts Him as her first priority—when any of us do—life seems to fall into place and line up. He is The Great I AM. He has the power to handle and fix anything, including a broken heart and a broken life.

Practical Tools

One of the practical tools I use is the "Letter from God" which can be found on www.fathersloveletter.com. There is the option to read the letter or watch the video. I use it as a tool to challenge how they see God and it's most effective with those that don't understand God's love for them. After they read or watch it, I ask them:

- Is that different than how you have been thinking of Him?
- What do you still have a hard time believing and why?
- Do you believe the Bible is true? Well then…is God a liar? Because this is right out of the Bible.

Another tool I use are the names of God, whether in a book or printed off the internet. I generally start with the ones they do not believe, which tells me a lot. It tells me what they do believe and helps me to ask more questions like, "What is it about that name that you don't believe?" It generally will point to an area she is stuck. For instance, she may say "Jehovah Nissi: God is My Protector. He didn't protect me when I was abused, so I don't believe that name is accurate."

#3 Get Unstuck

So if the Son sets you free, you will be free indeed.

—John 8:36

Description

Most people I have mentored have a firm belief that they are all messed up. I say to them "No, you're just a little stuck." There are those rare occasions, however, where I meet people who don't think they're stuck at all—and I enjoy showing them where they're wrong. No matter where you are in your walk with Him, you can always get a little more freed up.

This is the freedom step. God desires total freedom for us. It's He who sets us free, but He does ask us to partner with Him through our own choices. Getting unstuck is a choice—healing is a choice, and *this step is taking an active role in your own freedom by choosing to partner with the Lord.*

In this section, you will learn the power and ability of a person's own choice to surrender, confess, repent, forgive, and accept. These are the steps to take to get free from the things that have held a person back. Most of this type of healing is about getting rid of the junk that is covering up a person's real identity. Once those things are gone, then you begin pouring back in.

Some people will say, "My past made me who I am!" My answer to that is "No....God made the real you. You made the rest. What He made was good enough. In fact, you were fearfully and wonderfully made. You just have a bunch of junk covering up the real you, so let's get rid of it."

You see, it's not about adding more to who you are; it's about uncovering more. People are always looking for the "to-do list" of all the things they need to add to who they are to be "better." However, ask yourself: what can you really do to improve on what the Lord has made?

People have all kinds of issues like:

- Addictions
- Bitterness
- Self-harm
- Marital problems
- Depression
- Anxiety

But these issues are not THE ISSUE—they are the *symptoms* of a deeper issue, an unresolved issue. Picture a tree with huge branches and leaves (symptoms) then there is the trunk, and then the roots (unresolved issues). Most people spend their time working on the symptoms like healing from the addiction, but I believe we should be spending that precious time working on what caused (root) the addiction.

If you've been really listening to their answers in steps one and two, then you will most likely know where they are stuck. People get stuck by unresolved issues, and can't seem to move past them. We need to help them find the issue and resolve it. Think of past hurts that are still hurting them; that are causing the symptoms in their life currently. Look for the situation, not just the feeling or symptom that came from the situation—this is personal to each person. ***The following list ARE NOT questions you ask, just things to look for.*** These are the big ones that people have a hard time moving past, they are the possible unresolved issues or roots.

- Abandonment
- Molestation
- Rape
- Divorce
- Abortion
- Bullying
- Abuse
- Adoption
- Unanswered Prayer
- Infidelity
- Prostitution
- Spiritual Abuse

Indications of Being Stuck

Here are some classic indications that point to where a person is stuck—the root cause of their current issues:

- Every time she talks about a certain situation, she tears up or gets agitated.
- She is ashamed or guilty about something in her past.

- Looping. She will repeat the same story over and over again (I don't mean when she tells her testimony, because that is different).
- Her body language does not match her words. "Oh, but I've let that go a long time ago. I forgave her." Her face and body language, however, tell you a different story.
- She keeps blaming someone else for how her life has turned out. It may appear that she is just complaining about that person.
- She doesn't include a certain part of her past (that you know about) in her testimony.
- She may say, "I can't believe I'm telling you this…I've never told anyone this. I actually forgot about it until just now."

Getting unstuck can happen in a very short amount of time. Even though a Girl has been dealing with something for years, it doesn't mean it has to take years to heal from it. Most people are stuck in one or two areas that are holding them back.

When it comes to helping a Girl get unstuck, you just work with what's on top—not everything. It's not about solving all her problems at once. It's about hearing what she is going through *now*, and trying to find the root cause—then helping her rip it out so her current issues (symptoms) will cease. When a Girl keeps sharing about her current issues, I get her to go deeper by asking a lot of questions.

- When did that start?
- What do you think caused you to start doing that in the first place?
- When did you lose your peace and joy?

Surrender

The whole goal of Purely His is to surrender our whole lives to Jesus and help others do the same.

You gave your heart to Jesus, but you never gave your *whole life* to Him. That is what you see in someone who is "on fire." They have given Him their whole life. Call it surrender, call it rededicating their life, but they truly went ALL-IN and their life has NEVER been the same.

Surrendering our lives and going all-in is a choice. Everyone is literally *one choice* away from being "on fire" too. It's one choice, and then we walk it out with action. There is, of course, a significant day when you surrender all—but it is not a one-time action. It is a lifestyle.

You say the words and hand it over to Him as an act of trust, which is faith in action. Trust isn't always a feeling—it's an action.

You want your Girls making the choice to surrender their lives to the Lord first—then they have the power and courage to do the hard work. Some people, however, just aren't willing to go all-in yet; you'll just have to be patient. Sometimes, they are not able to go all-in with Jesus until they forgive Him for what they perceive He did wrong.

THIS is where a Girl can go from lukewarm to HOT with one single choice.

Surrender those things you are worried about, anxious of, or *concerned* about. We all have ways of disguising our worry or anxiety, because we know that it is wrong, but being *concerned* sounds so responsible doesn't it? We think it is our responsibility.

Choose to surrender your past, present and future mistakes. It's important to surrender your dreams too. Learn to place your whole life in His hands EVERY day. Worrying is a lack of trusting in the Lord. LEARN to trust Him in everything. Let me remind you of this: *trust isn't always a feeling—it's an action.*

- What are you holding onto that the Lord wants you to let go of?
- Have you ever given your whole life to Jesus?

Surrender is very freeing. It gets rid of the junk covering up the real you, which is holding you back.

DO NOT push this part. Put it out there, and see if she'll make the choice—if not now, then later. Surrendering to Jesus is THE ANSWER to ALL her unresolved issues being healed.

ALL-IN

In order to follow Jesus with all your heart—and to teach others to do the same—you need to go "ALL-IN" first. It's important that you surrender your entire life to Him and truly follow Him. "Follow me as I follow Christ." Point them toward Him *through your life*. Be filled up by Him and it will automatically pour out of you. Turn believers into followers by being a follower yourself. The goal of Purely His is for you to surrender your whole life to Jesus. This is where you decide if you're ready to GO ALL-IN with Jesus or if you want to keep going around the same mountain for a while.

- This is where we decide, "Not my will, but Yours, Lord." I'm going to put my whole life in your hands—past, present, and future. I'm done doing life on my own; I want and need your help. So here you go. Here's my life."
- Surrender your worry and anxious thoughts concerning you. Worrying is lack of trust in the Lord.
- Surrender your past, present and future mistakes to Him.
- Surrender your dreams of the future to Him.
- Learn to place your whole life in His hands EVERY day.
- Surrender is an **act** or willingness to begin to trust. It's not a **feeling.** The more you live it out in action, the more you will be able to trust Him and others. Surrender. It gets rid of the junk that is covering up the real you.

But seek first his kingdom and his righteousness, and all these things will be given to you as well.

— Matthew 6:33

Confession

... confess your sins to each other and pray for each other so that you may be healed.

— James 5:16a

When things are in the dark (secret) that's where the Enemy has a field day with us. Confession brings it to the light where Jesus is. It can only be healed when brought to the Healer. This is a natural process that usually doesn't need much prompting, because it happens naturally in Steps One and Two. Most people love to talk about themselves, and that has already been happening in your relationship.

This is where you need to be paying close attention: *they will usually confess where they are stuck if you listen closely enough*. You can recognize a confession by how they say it:

- I can't believe I'm telling you this
- I've never told anyone this before
- I forgot all about this

Confession is such a relief to the person who has been holding onto it for a long time. But then the "buyer's remorse" usually kicks in. They may say something like, "I am regretting saying too much to you."

Some people might say:

"I can't stop crying.... I didn't cry when it happened, so why am I crying now?"

My explanation:

"I believe it is years of tears...healing tears. It wasn't safe to cry then—you had to survive. Now it's time to heal."

If someone is having a hard time confessing, and you know there is more than what they have shared, then say something like:

- Do you have anything hidden that needs to come to the light and be healed?
- I won't judge you.

Dropping Bombs

I want to help you *respond*—versus *react*—to confessions that are hard to hear. It's very difficult for a Girl to humble herself and share a secret with you or a group—so handle it ever so delicately.

Imagine yourself mentoring a Girl who says one of these things to you. *Please pay attention to your **facial expressions** as you read these real-life confessions* (listed below) made by Girls whom I have worked with (and some are my own confessions).

- *My dad was a pastor, so I was at church all the time growing up. Another pastor sexually abused me for many years...he made me call him Jesus, and thank him for cleansing me*
- *I have had sex with over one hundred people*
- *My dad started having sex with me around the age of eleven, and it's still going on; I'm afraid to tell my mom...is it weird that I still love him?*
- *I sexually abused someone...just like it was done to me*
- *I have had eight abortions, and I'm pregnant again*
- *I'm dating a married man, but he is going to leave his wife; he doesn't love her anymore*
- *I used to sell naked pictures of myself online to pay my bills*
- *My mom used to make me do sexual things with her and her boyfriends*

Handling What You Hear

1. What Does Your Face Look Like?

This is the most important thing! When working with Girls, you need to brace yourself for very hard-to-hear confessions. Try not to be surprised. Try not to have a disgusted look on your face. She is going to be watching your body language and your eyes very intently. *She wants to know if you will judge her or abandon her after.*

2. Reassure and Encourage Her

Thank her for her trust in you. She took the biggest step, ***confession***, which is bringing it from the dark (where Satan is) and moved it to the light (where God can heal it). She is well on her way to healing. The Bible says, *confess your sins to each other and pray for each other so that you may be healed* (James 5:16a).

3. Wrong or Ineffective Response (Versus Effective)

An Ineffective Response:

"Oh…I know EXACTLY how you feel."

Although you *think* you TOTALLY know and feel what she is feeling, her circumstance is unique. Yes, you can relate, but not perfectly. Therefore, try to back off of the words TOTALLY and EXACTLY. It lessens her pain—invalidates it—when you *think* you *totally* understand. The situation is similar, not *exactly* the same.

An Effective Response:

"I can relate, I remember feeling similar to that. But Jesus can relate to being abandoned, rejected, hurt, abused, betrayed…."

You always want to pull Jesus back into the conversation. Make sure she knows *that you had help*—and still do. You want to help her get closer to Him.

Caution:

If you can't relate, ***don't act like you can****. It's offensive.*

4. What Are You Thinking?

Be mindful and careful of the thoughts you're thinking—they are guaranteed to show on your face.

You may be shocked or horrified. It's best to be in constant prayer in your head. Ask the Lord to help you know what to do. Ask for His perspective, His wisdom, and His compassion.

5. What Do You Do with it Personally after You've Heard It?

It is very important to surrender *all confessions by others* to the Lord. It is not our weight to bear. The Lord says: *Come unto Me all who are weary or heavily burdened and I will give you rest* (Matthew 11:28). These are heavy burdens; do not shoulder them alone.

These types of confessions also come with *explicit mental images* that you need to surrender to the Lord. You also may need to get someone to pray over you without sharing the specific details of her confession.

For instance—because my past is full of sex, I have to be careful when dealing with a Girl who is struggling. The mental pornographic images I worked so hard to get rid of…try to come back. Knowing this, I will call my mentor or talk to my husband and ask them to pray over me. That always does the trick for me.

Without divulging details, I tell them:

"I talked with a Girl today, and there were some things shared that are triggering me—mostly in the sexual department. Can you please pray over me?"

The other thing I do is ***take every thought captive*** (2 Corinthians 10:5). I do not ponder the explicit images or thoughts; I quickly dismiss them. They are not coming from me—so I don't claim them as mine.

6. How Should You Handle It?

Depending on the confession, you will have different results.

Caution:

*If she is a **minor**, and a crime is being committed, then you have a duty to tell authorities.*

If it is a crime that happened in the past, *and she's not in danger*, then you can take a little more time. It is always good, however, for her to confront those things by standing up for herself and telling someone, whether it is a parent or the authorities. When a situation arises like this…you cannot keep a promise like "I won't tell anyone."

Don't make promises you can't keep.

Often, people will ask you to make that promise prior to the confession—so be careful not to agree to it. Give yourself an out by saying:

"I won't tell anyone unless you are in danger."

If you did make a promise without giving yourself the "out," however, then you will have to go back on your word ***for your own protection and hers***. We are responsible for what we know.

7. How Do You Walk Them Through It?

No matter how big the sin is on her part—or someone else's—the method to healing is still the same. The steps still work.

Forgiveness is not just for small things; it works the same way no matter how big the issue is. If it is criminal in nature, charges may need to be pressed, or restraining orders need to be put in place. In this case, I would ask someone who would have that answer for you.

Forgiveness

Forgiveness is the cornerstone of our faith as Christians. Without it, we wouldn't have the opportunity to have relationships with God.

"You can't give what you don't have."

— Steve Siebold

It is the same in the spiritual realm. You can't give love, if you haven't received it. You cannot forgive, unless you have been forgiven—in other words, you have to *receive* forgiveness. The truth is, if you are a Christian, then you have been forgiven of EVERY sin you have committed—and will commit.

The question you have to answer:

*Have you truly received the forgiveness that Jesus has given **you**?*

Receive Forgiveness:

If you don't FEEL forgiven, then maybe you need to receive (accept) His forgiveness again for something specific. He says that if you ask, He will give it (1 John 1:9), but sometimes we aren't really good at receiving.

Forgiveness is a free gift that God offers. We do not need to earn it; we just need to receive it. You may not *feel* forgiven, but the truth is—*you are*.

Geoffrey Chaucer wrote, "Time heals all wounds." I disagree. *Time* doesn't heal all wounds—*resolving issues* does. Forgiveness is the GREATEST way to resolve issues. This is where we partner with the Healer: Jesus Christ.

Forgiveness is a choice. It is not a feeling. You will *never* feel like forgiving someone—especially for a horrendous crime. *But it is possible*...especially when you take the time to dwell on everything you have personally been forgiven for.

Un-forgiveness is a sin. If you forgive those that have hurt you—including God and yourself—the symptoms of bitterness will go away, and Satan will have nothing to hold on to.

Keep in mind: the Lord does not distinguish between which sins we are to forgive and which ones we aren't (or should take our sweet time forgiving). He simply says, *forgive as I have forgiven you* (Colossians 3:13; Ephesians 4:32; Matthew 6:14).

Let's Review:

FIRST: *Receive forgiveness*

THEN: *Give it away*

Give Forgiveness Away:

When someone does something to hurt you—whether they meant to or not—they offended you. You need to forgive them, or else bitterness starts to take root—*in YOU*. Bitterness is often referred to as *cancer of the soul* because it eats away at you, and causes all kinds of problems, especially in relationships. Forgiveness is not a feeling; it's an action, and we are commanded to do it—it's a sin if we don't.

You will never FEEL like forgiving your husband...or a man who raped or molested you...and you will definitely never FEEL like forgiving yourself. ***But you really need to***. It will set you free in so many ways. Bitterness never goes away on its own, it just keeps collecting more. Forgiveness will get rid of it.

- **Forgiveness** *doesn't mean that "it" never happened*
- **Forgiveness** *doesn't excuse the bad behavior of another*
- **Forgiveness** *doesn't mean what happened wasn't wrong*
- **Forgiveness** *is **not for them***
- **Forgiveness** *is for **you** and **your relationship with Jesus***

If you love Me, do what I command.

— Jesus *(John 14:15)*

Review the Process of Forgiveness:

- Receive forgiveness
- Forgive God
- Forgive others
- Forgive yourself

Ask yourself these questions:

- What do you need to ask forgiveness for?
- What holds you back from receiving forgiveness from Jesus?
- Who do you need to forgive?
- What do you need to forgive (others) for?
- What is holding you back from forgiving them?

Picture this:

When someone hurts you—and you don't forgive him or her right away—that incident is hooked onto you, and you begin dragging it through life with you. Think of all the people you have been dragging—who are hooked to your back *right now*. Aren't they getting heavy?

Here's what you do:

Unhook them from you.

Hook them to God.

Now they owe Him, not you anymore. You are lighter, and you are free—no longer being dragged down by the hooks of bitterness from your past.

Forgive, for the Father forgave you.

— Colossians 3:13; Ephesians 4:32; Matthew 6:14 (paraphrase)

Some say it's sacrilegious to forgive God, but I say if you have a personal relationship with Him, and you have something against Him...**He *already knows* what you have against Him. He wants more than anything to be close to you.** So get whatever it is out of the way; then you can be close again.

Forgiving God is the same process; only He will not owe Himself afterward ;-). You unhook that "offense" from you, hand it to Him, while making the choice to not hold that offense against Him again. The greatest benefit to doing this is your relationship with Him will be restored, because there will not be anything in between your relationsip anymore. The gap will be closed.

Forgiveness is choosing to never hold a specific record of wrongs against another. I believe forgiveness needs to be done out loud, and it needs to be specific—so the Enemy can hear you. Satan holds onto areas of our life where sin, like bitterness, is present. This is one way you *defeat him*, and force him to *let go* of this area.

Real Life Example: *How I Pray a Prayer of Forgiveness*

Lord,

Thank you so much for forgiving me for everything.... thank you for forgiving me for the abortions I had, for using drugs all those years, for neglecting my boys for the attention of men, for lying, stealing, and cheating.

I know I don't deserve your forgiveness, but you gave it to me anyway, and Lord I receive it right now. When I remind myself of what I have been forgiven for, it makes it easier for me to forgive others.

I know that you ask me to forgive those who have hurt me, and forgive others as you have forgiven me, so that's what I'm going to do.

Lord, I choose to forgive that guy [I use his real name when

I'm actually forgiving] for raping me. That day changed my life, and hurt me so deeply. It continues to hurt me now. So Lord, I am unhooking him from me, and I am hooking him to you. He no longer owes me anything—he owes you now.

And Lord, I ask you to heal me from the hurt that his choice caused me. I don't want to hurt anymore.

Lord, I also want to pray for him, but I don't have the strength or words without you.... Would you bless him by helping him to ***find you and give his life to you****? Have mercy on his soul.*

Amen.

Real Life Example: *Brief Introduction of a Man Who Forgave Himself*

My husband, Matt, has a Guy in his group who is also a childhood friend. This man went into the military right after high school, and he fought in the war in Afghanistan.

That war really messed him up: he lost his marriage because his wife was unfaithful; he lost several of his friends in battle; his health has declined due to a grenade exploding near him, and he was severely traumatized by survivor's guilt.

He had been in charge of a platoon—*and he was the only survivor*. This gave him all kinds of problems. He had nightmares, he contemplated suicide, and he felt ashamed in front of the Lord, his family, and the other soldiers in the military. *He was stuck.*

Matt: I've noticed that when we're in group—you seem to tell the same story over and over again. Why are you choosing to pack around that guilt with you all the time? Jesus died to pay for your mistakes and sins. Why are you trying to pay for them?

Guy: What am I supposed to do? I don't deserve forgiveness for them dying on my watch. I have been carrying around this burden—this guilt—for years, and I feel like I am supposed to.

Matt: *No one* deserves forgiveness. That's the beauty of His grace—it's unearned and undeserved. The Lord wants to set you free from the guilt you're carrying around. It's time that you forgave yourself.

Guy: Why should I do that?

Matt: Firstly, you're miserable. Secondly, if you forgive yourself—*and are set free from the torment of the guilt and shame*—how many veterans could you help do the same? You see, that is your circle of influence…those are your people, your assignments from God.

Guy: You actually think that God would want to use me to help others like that?

Matt: Absolutely! You are *perfect* for the job. He wants to put you back on the front lines, only this time you are fighting with and for the Army of the Lord.

Guy: That gives me so much hope…thank you, Matt. How do I do it?

Matt: Let's pray it out together, right now. Forgiveness is a choice. You can make that choice right now. Then we'll pray it out together over the phone—and you'll be free. *All you're doing is taking the gift that God has given you already, and choosing to give it to yourself.*

They prayed it out together—*right there on the phone*—and immediately his guilt and shame was removed from him. He is so excited that the Lord wants to use him to reach other men and women who are in bondage to the horrific side effects of survivor's guilt. We look forward to seeing how the Lord will be using this man of God!

What to Expect

Everyone has different reactions immediately following forgiveness—*because our bodies weren't made for that amount of stress and bitterness*. Most people feel very relieved, some feel nauseous, others get migraines, and a few get really tired and need a nap. No way is wrong; people are just different. Some people cry really hard while they're forgiving, and some people don't cry at all. Forgiveness is not about emotion—it's about making a choice to do something that is really hard to do.

Get to the point where you have forgiven EVERYONE. And then as new hurts happen, forgive quickly. You are going to love how you feel ***after*** you forgive. It doesn't feel good during. The Enemy will try and trick you that you didn't really mean it, and say to you "if you meant it, then why are you still hurt over it?" You may still have hurt feelings, but God will heal those too.

Repentance

Therefore, since we have these promises, dear friends, let us purify ourselves from everything that contaminates body and spirit, perfecting holiness out of reverence for God.

— 2 Corinthians 7:1

Repentance is a part of surrender. You choose to surrender your sin and go toward the Lord and His ways. It equals trust and faith—without it, we cannot please God (Hebrews 11:6). Ask Him to help with your unbelief (Mark 9:24). He is the One who gives us faith in the first place (Ephesians 2:8), so ask Him for more of it.

The reason we need to choose to purify ourselves is because we are living in the end times. We need to teach people to be ready… ready to run to Him and not shrink back. We all need to repent from our wicked ways, because the kingdom of God is near (2 Chronicles 7:14; Matthew 3:2).

Repentance is making a choice to turn away from sin and ***turn toward the Lord***. It is, *with the help of the Lord*, stopping what we know to be sin. When we focus on the Lord—instead of the sin—it is very helpful.

Here are a couple of examples:

If a Girl wants to quit drugs, she shouldn't constantly look at the drugs and say to herself, "Try not to think about drugs…try not to think about drugs." All she is doing is focusing on the drugs *more*. It's much easier and better for her, to take her eyes off the sin (in this case, drugs) and focus on Jesus instead. The more she moves toward Him, the farther she moves away from sin.

Encourage her toward what ***to do***, not toward what ***not to do***.

But seek first his kingdom and his righteousness, and all these things will be given to you as well.

— Matthew 6:33

If a Girl is always focusing on "Don't think about sex…don't think about sex." What is she thinking about? Instead, teach her to *think about Jesus…think about Jesus*! When she moves toward Jesus, she'll automatically move away from sin.

Fasting is a practical tool that really helps. God never tells us to do something that He doesn't give us the power to pull off. Don't buy "I can't stop watching porn; I just can't." Bull. *Choose* to stop. *Choose* to repent. Allow the God of the universe to help you make a *new* habit. Break the addiction. Note: Those who are still struggling with eating disorders should choose to fast from something other than food, such as Facebook, coffee or TV.

Submit yourselves, then, to God. Resist the devil, and he will flee from you.

— James 4:7

Questions I Use to Get to the Heart of the Matter

- We are all tempted by different sins…which one tempts you?
- What sin are you currently struggling with?

Acceptance

As you walked your Girl through these steps, she got rid of a bunch of stuff—*emptied*—now it's time to fill her back up. **She needs to accept the truths about herself**. Once the junk is gone, the filter is clean. She can begin accepting good things back in; healthy things. Truth and Love. *Accepting* means pouring back into HER—while realizing her true identity.

It is really hard for a Girl to know her true identity when a bunch of junk is covering up the real her. She must allow the Lord to love her and others to love her. She must choose to accept forgiveness and grace.

Jesus came to set the captives free (Luke 4:18), and it is *His truth that sets us free* (John 8:32), but we don't have to choose to receive it. Those who do, however, *will be free indeed*.

#4 Walk It Out

As a prisoner for the Lord, then, I urge you to live a life worthy of the calling you have received. —Ephesians 4:1

Description

Faith is *believing in something* we cannot see. Faith is an action, not just a feeling. All the time, I hear Girls say:

I know it up here (pointing to her head), but I don't KNOW it in here (pointing to her heart).

The way you get it **from your head to your heart** is by DOING it. Walk it out. The Bible is clear: *be doers of the word, not hearers only* (James 1:22, ESV).

Without actually *doing* what it says, it's pretty hard to *learn* it. Doing it makes it her own and will help her really learn it.

Now faith is confidence in what we hope for and assurance about what we do not see.

— Hebrews 11:1 (emphasis mine)

This is her *TRUE identity.*

She is free. Now, she has to learn ***how to walk it out.*** She read it. Believed it. Accepted it. Now it's time to practice it. She can stumble through this life in her true identity, getting comfortable with it—owning it. It's much easier to be true to yourself, once you realize who you are and practice being authentic for a time.

WALK OUT your own salvation...

—Philippians 2:12 (paraphrase)

This is her *BIBLICAL identity.*

She may FEEL like it's not true. When she learns to walk in the truth and not her feelings, eventually her feelings will match the truth. As humans, we get so caught up in the habit of *fear and insecurity*—that it becomes second nature. We are being commanded to make a **new habit.**

This step is where the *rubber meets the road*—belief, not feelings, meeting action.

Does she really believe what she's been learning about herself and the Lord? *Now faith is being sure of what we hope for and certain of what we do not see* (Hebrews 11:1, NIV/1989). Faith is believing in something we **cannot** see. Faith is an action, not necessarily a feeling. This step is where we help her to REALLY KNOW it.

The Best Way to Do This:

Just do it!

Show her when you learn something new in the Bible, or from church, or someone challenges you. *Just get out and do it!* Even if it doesn't make sense; even if it looks foolish, like praying for a building you cannot afford. It's how you will actually learn it. It's how you get something from your head to your heart.

Encourage your Girls to **walk it out**—whether they are new to faith, or have been Believers for a long time (those are the toughest).

WALK OUT:

- New truths
- Calling
- Repentance
- Decisions
- Faith
- Professed beliefs

Your Girl needs to hear she is no longer surviving; she has *survived*—so now, she can walk in freedom. Fruit keeps with repentance. If she truly repented, her life (actions) will prove her choice. You have gone first in these steps. How does repentance look in your life? Share how it looked to walk out of your old lifestyle and into your new identity and new relationship with the Lord.

When I was struggling through an anxious situation, this is a word the Lord gave to me. I hope it is an encouragement to you as well:

This is the way; now walk in it.
I AM the Way, the Truth, and the Life.
Walk toward Me. Walk in Me. Walk for Me.

The Heart of the Matter: *Questions to Ask Yourself, Then Your Girls*

- What steps will you take to walk in total dependence on the Lord?

- From now on, how will your life begin to look different?
- What new truth have you have learned about *yourself* or *God* that has set you free?
- What will your fully-surrendered life look like from now on?
- What area in your life are you still having a hard time *believing*, but you're going to *walk it out* anyway?

Real Life Example

For several years, I have known a single mom who is in her fifties. She has nine kids (yes, I said *nine* kids). I have had the privilege of mentoring her and her five daughters.

When I met her, this mom was a strong Believer in the Lord. She had been through trials in life that most of us would crumble under. She came from an alcoholic home growing up, lived an adventurous life in her twenties, and experienced the heartache of breakups with boyfriends and the shame of many mistakes.

She gave her life to the Lord in her early twenties, and wanted to do things right. She didn't meet men in the ways she used to—instead, she met a man at Bible study, and they got married very quickly. She believed he was *the one*. What she didn't realize about this "godly" man was that he was an alcoholic, an emotional abuser, and a sex addict.

They decided to trust God with everything—including birth control, and had one kid every eighteen months. After years of agony being married to this man, she proceeded with a divorce. All of the kids had issues of some sort, and the house was in absolute chaos. They spent years trying to recover. Through counseling, mentoring—and just their stubborn determination never to give up—they are all doing so much better. The Lord has seen them through. She has no help with the kids, or child support from her ex-husband.

I received a panicked phone call from her recently, and this is how it went:

Girl: I can't do this anymore (as she sobbed uncontrollably). They want me to do all this stuff at work that I don't know how to do. I feel so inadequate, and I just want to quit. Plus, the kids need me to take them to doctors and dentists appointments… my house is a mess, and my van is about to break down again.

Me: Wow…that is a lot on your plate. Let me pray for you:

"Lord, your daughter is tired and weak right now; she needs your wisdom and strength to pull this one off. You said *come unto Me all you who are weary and heavy burdened and I will give you rest* (Matthew 11:28), and Lord, she needs your rest right now. So we're coming to You for help. Please comfort her. Remind her who she is in You; give me the words to help her right now on Your behalf."

Girl: Thanks for praying, Michelle. Sometimes, it just helps to say this stuff out loud. I'm so overwhelmed with everything. It's too much.

Me: It's too much for anyone to handle, but WITH the Lord, ALL things are possible. It sounds like you got a little off-track, and have been doing all of this in your own strength—and frankly, that's impossible. So my first encouragement to you is to *return to your first love* (Revelation 2:4) and have Him help you with all of this. Secondly, I want you to get out a piece of paper right now—as we're talking—and write a list of all the things that you are stressing about. It will help you get it out of your head and onto paper. Then, I'll help you prioritize your list. Okay?

Girl: Okay. I really have been trying to do this all on my own. I don't know why I always leave the Lord…and then wonder why life is so hard.

Me: Well, because the world we live in tells us we need to be strong, independent, women—and the Lord says just the opposite. *My strength is made perfect in your weakness* (2 Corinthians 12:9). He's fine with our weaknesses, and He totally wants to help us. Remember that *He is an ever-present help in time of need* (Psalm 46:1).

Girl: I totally know those scriptures as truth; I just haven't been living like that.

Me: I know you know all of this; I'm reminding you of the truth that will set you free. Like Paul said, *It is no trouble for me to write the same things to you again, and it is a safeguard for you* (Philippians 3:1). I remind, and then you walk it out. Take what you believe and apply it right now. That's walking it out. Write the list, and then complete it WITH the Lord. He wants to help you do everything—even laundry.

Girl: Thank you so much for listening to me freak out. I think the thing that was bothering me was that I felt alone. Thank you for reminding me the Lord is with me and will help me.

I helped her write her list, and then prioritize it. Sometimes, mentoring is practical life-help, mixed with the spiritual. But it is *always* important to point her to Jesus, not yourself. She came to me for help, but had first turned her back to the Lord, her Helper.

My final words to her: *You are more than a conqueror. You are the famous single mom of nine kids. You got this! Remember who you are, and* ***walk it out****.*

Literally Walk It Out

When we first learn something, it's important to ***start walking it out right away***. Then, we never forget, and we can learn it at a deeper level. **This takes it from knowing it in our minds, to knowing it in our hearts.** It becomes a part of us.

Our number-one goal is to continue growing in Christ, becoming more like Him. As we discussed, ***walking it out*** does just that. I also like to walk it out *literally*.

Praise Walk

A Praise Walk is praying out loud with a purpose. I do this with my Girls one-on-one or in a group. They can do this individually with the Lord as well. It doesn't have to be formal, or even a real "walk"…it can happen while someone is alone in the shower, the car, while cooking, cleaning, or journaling a list of praises.

When you are down and need a pick-me-up, then *praise the Lord*. Learn to praise Him in everything—especially when things aren't going the way you would want them to. It blesses the Lord's heart when you appreciate what He has and is doing for you.

- List **out loud** the things you are thankful for
- Watch how quickly your mood changes
- It will help you remember God is good
    - He's come through for you all those other times
    - Why wouldn't He now?

Satan hates it when we praise God, he wants us to ignore or curse Him. Can you imagine what would happen if *every time* you were attacked by Satan, you *praised* God instead? That would teach him not to mess with you!

Surrender Walk

A Surrender Walk is a good walk for those times where the burdens feel very heavy. Jesus told us *come all you who are weary and heavily burdened and I will give you rest* (Matthew 11:28). From the little stuff to the big stuff, give it to Him until you feel relief.

> "Lord, I am so stressed out right now. I give you all these things that are bothering me. Even though I don't feel I can let go, I am deciding to trust you. I choose to take the step and lay it before you, and ask you for the strength to let it go into your hands."

Intercessory Walk

An Intercessory Walk is not only an excellent walk for learning to lift one another up in prayer (James 5:16, Galatians 6:2), but it is also good for the Girl who is self-centered or depressed—**because she needs to focus on others** (Philippians 2:3-4). The more someone focuses on others, the happier they will be.

Prayer Example

"Lord, I am so used to focusing on myself and all my problems, but today I'm going to turn my attention and thoughts towards others and their needs. I just want to lift up Susie and ask that you would bless her with finances because I know she's struggling financially and could really use the help. Lord, I also want to pray blessings over my neighbor with Cancer, he really needs You to comfort him today as he is in a lot of pain. Lord, when I look at everyone else's problems, it makes mine seem so small. Thank you for all you're doing in my life!"

Real Life Example:

I have a dream of having Purely His Mentoring Centers all over the place. Last week, I went to a Biblical class at my church where we were studying prayer. We were using a book called *The Circle Maker* by Mark Batterson. The author based his book on the story of Jericho, and how they ***prayerfully walked*** around the walls for seven days—and the walls fell.

In one part of his personal story, Batterson says, "I will not allow my budget to determine my dreams." And *bam*, it hit me. I have been waiting until I CAN provide enough money to dream about having these centers. I need to be trusting in the Lord to *be my provider—my Jehovah Jireh*—and start asking him to make these walls FALL.

The very next day, my new friend and I started **walking** around that building (which costs $800,000—*crazy*) and we were asking the Lord to provide it for our ministry. Now keep in mind…I had zero money to throw at this—I was only making $600 a month at the time, so in the natural—that was ridiculous. However, *NOTHING is impossible for God* (Luke 1:37).

I didn't wait until it made sense—I acted on what I heard. I was struggling with unbelief at that point, but I chose not to give up. I chose to keep knocking, keep asking, and keep **walking** it out.

STEP FIVE: *Take Someone with You*

...first take the plank out of your own eye, **and then** *you will see clearly to remove the speck from your brother's eye.*

— *Matthew 7:5* (*emphasis mine*)

Description

Step five is a natural progression. Your Girl has learned so many new things—and they've worked! Now it's time to encourage her to share it with someone else. Teach her to take what she's learned, and pass it on by bringing someone along with her…this is where it gets SO fun! We are all supposed to be doing it…*this is our calling* (Matthew 28:19).

The whole time you are mentoring, it's important you keep in mind that **you are never above those you mentor**…*consider others better than yourself* (Philippians 2:3). Ask her for prayer sometime. Find a strength of hers that is a weakness of your own and allow her to mentor you. Don't pretend like you have it all together, you don't. None of us do.

We have a tendency to wear a mask that looks more spiritual or holy than we actually are. It's also important for them to know what your current struggles are, and how you overcome them. Be a real person, not someone in a place they can never reach or achieve.

Not that I have already obtained all this, or have already arrived at my goal*, but I press on to take hold of that for which Christ Jesus took hold of me. Brothers and sisters, I do not consider myself yet to have taken hold of it. But one thing I do: Forgetting what is behind and straining toward what is ahead,* ***I press on toward the goal to win the prize for which God has called me heavenward in Christ Jesus.***

— *Philippians 3:12-14*

Jesus told us we ***will do greater things than he has done*** (John 14:12) because we have His Spirit working in and through us. We are to follow His ways of mentoring—and encourage those we mentor that ***they can also do greater things than Him.***

Opportunities to Let Your Girls Pass You Up and/or Help Them Start Mentoring:

- Buy her this book so she can copy what you did with her
- Ask for her input on a situation with another Girl, or her advice when mentoring someone whom she can better relate to
- Have her involved in a mentoring session with you and another Girl (with the other Girl's permission)

The Heart of the Matter

These questions can help her start thinking about how she can begin taking someone with her.

- How are you going to begin serving?
- Name three people you are going to invite to a Christian function
- How and where are you going to share your testimony?

Real Life Example

One of my very dear friends is on the pastoral staff at her church, and also works with junior high students. She gave me a call, and it went something like this:

Friend: Hey there, so after three years, I've decided to quit doing the Junior High Ministry.

Me: Oh wow, that's exciting! Who have you been mentoring to take your place?

Friend: What do you mean? I just figured that when I quit, then someone will have to just...*step up* and take my place.

Me: Oh no you don't. If you leave and don't replace yourself, most likely that ministry will die. This is why a lot of churches are dying out—lack of discipleship.

Friend: I never thought of that, I just figured...

Me: Let me guess, you're planning on putting a call out through your bulletin: "We are in need of a leader for the Junior High Ministry. Who wants to volunteer?"

Friend: Exactly, how did you know?

Me: It won't work. How did Jesus teach others to disciple and lead? He didn't ask for volunteers; He would walk up to someone and say, "Hey you, follow me." And they did. He hand-picked people—so we should do the same.

Friend: I can't believe I didn't think about this before. What do I do now?

Me: I would pray about three people who you should be training to take your place. Then invite them to start helping out. We should always be thinking about replacing ourselves. We shouldn't ever be doing ministry alone.

Friend: Our church leadership needs to adopt this line of thinking. I don't think any of us are doing this. Will you come and teach us at our leadership retreat coming up?

Me: Absolutely, I would love that!

Following this conversation, I was invited to attend their church's leadership retreat just a couple months later. The Lord used me to fan their fire again for discipleship/mentoring. Also, my husband and I were later invited to share our hearts for discipleship with the whole congregation. This was the first church that decided to financially support us. The Lord is amazing!

Practical Tools for You and Your Girls

- Give her an opportunity to tell her testimony on a stage, one-on-one, or in a blog
- Encourage her to invite someone to church, Bible study or special church event
- Start a Sisterhood in her home or church
- Take someone else through the 5 Steps
- Give her opportunities to lead
- Encourage and mentor each other within a group atmosphere

- Proclaim your faith and story on social media
- Learn to serve each other and together
    - *Jesus came to serve, not be served* (Matthew 20:28)
    - He served out of a full cup from the Father, and so should we
- One Girl takes another Girl to coffee while the rest of the Sisterhood cleans her house
- The Purely His Band of Brothers drives to the local Rescue Mission and shares their stories with the men there while they share a meal with them

CHAPTER 7—WARNINGS

Mentoring the Opposite Gender

We believe that men should mentor men and women should mentor women. *Older men teach the younger men—Older women teach the younger women* (Titus 2). I am not saying that a man cannot speak into a woman's life, but it is done most appropriately when their spouse is present or another person. A lot of complications and temptations come when you mentor across gender lines—especially if the topics are pertaining to relationships or sexuality. Stick with your own kind.

Save the Relationship at All Costs

Tell her what you think. If she decides against what you are suggesting, **respect her decision and support her as a person** (not her decision and/or choices).

> I have a Girl in her mid-twenties who wanted to serve the Lord with everything in her, but she was still holding onto a huge part of her former ways and identity—one of which was that she was dating a guy in prison, and was going to wait for him for six years. The relationship was unhealthy to begin with, and it continued to be.
>
> Both of their families were completely against them being together as a couple—and so was I, but I decided not to jump on that bandwagon, because it wasn't going to be effective at that time. Everyone else was coming against it, so I didn't have to.
>
> My main goal was to get her to the place of making the choice to go *all-in* with Jesus. I kept building my relationship with her and pointing her to the Lord. Later on, she asked what I thought about him. I was able to "use her own words

against her" and the different ways the Lord had spoken to her about the relationship. After our conversation, she ended that relationship and has been free from him for several months.

If I had given her my opinion right up front—and joined everyone else—it would not have helped anything. I needed to be strategic in "keeping the main thing the main thing" as Stephen R. Covey says. I knew that if she went all-in with Jesus, then *He* would convict her heart, and it would make it easy for her to receive my advice to leave her boyfriend. **I needed to save my relationship with her at all costs.**

"Sometimes, by losing a battle, you find a new way to win the war."

— Donald Trump

I waited till she asked what I thought about the situation. By that time, I knew her well enough, and I could use her *own words against her.* I was able to show her that even *she* didn't think he was right for her. I also used words from her own story where she distinctly heard God telling her that he wanted her to stay single.

If a Girl is in an unhealthy situation—like the sex industry or an abusive relationship—and you have shared your heart and concern with her, then you need to keep your comments to yourself and continue your relationship (unless she is a minor, we are never to leave them in danger and not do anything). She knows how you feel now. Your opinions, concerns, and beliefs are on the table—so keep them there, but don't force her to listen to you nag her. It's ineffective.

She will need a hand to grab when she's ready to come out of that situation. If you save the relationship at all costs, then your hand will be the one she reaches for. *If at all possible*, I think it's wise not to completely sever the relationship with the abuser either, so that you can keep your relationship intact with her, because he can stop her from communicating with you. I call this *strategic grace*.

When dealing with a Girl you're mentoring, or even your daughter in this type of situation—*you need to make it about her*. It's not about you. Pity parties don't work when trying to make a Girl change her mind. There is a time and place for emotions, but too many moms or mentors take it personally and make it personal—*this is not about you*! So keep your emotions to a minimum, and keep your head in the game. Be smart and strategic when dealing with her and those around her. You can break down emotionally behind closed doors.

Buyer's Remorse

She may ask if what she's feeling is normal. A lot of times Girls will have what I call *buyer's remorse* where she regrets telling you more than she planned. This is where shame enters, and fear sets in—mostly fear of judgment and rejection. When this happens, **and it usually happens**, I just keep it real and call it out.

Me: Thank you for sharing those details about your life with me. I know when I share big things with new people…I tend to get *buyer's remorse* where I regret telling them vulnerable stuff, and wish I could take it back. Mostly, because I'm not sure what they are going to think about me now. Are you feeling that way at all?

Girl: Yes.

Me: [comforting her] I don't feel any different about you as far as negatively. In fact, I'm *really proud of you* for all that you've endured and still survived. And I feel closer to you now that we've both shared our stories with each other.

Or I might say…

Me: Hey, just to give you a head's up…it's totally normal to have *buyer's remorse* after sharing all your junk with me/us. I know this from personal experience. I just want to let you know that it's normal to feel that way, but also, I think you're a really cool chick, and it amazes me how much you've gone through, and you never gave up. Wow, I'm glad we met!

When She Turns on You

There will come a point where you will go from being the *most awesome person* to the *target of her pain*. After the honeymoon phase is over, the true colors (the ugly ones) will show, and you will see what her family and friends have been complaining about. HANG IN THERE…this too shall pass.

Her true colors are about to bring out yours—so hold on. They may force you to begin having pretend arguments with her when you are alone in your house, "Listen here little lady…." This is usually brought on by you telling or advising her to do something she doesn't want to do, or you might be hitting the "mom trigger" because most of these Girls have parent issues.

She could be pushing the boundaries to see if you will leave her, because in her mind, *everyone leaves at some point*. She might also be self-sabotaging, because she doesn't believe in herself. **She needs you now more than ever**. Do NOT give up on her. Give her a little space, PRAY, and then text her or message her on Facebook. Let her know that you love her, you believe in her, and you aren't going anywhere.

Call for backup when you need it. Call your Mentor to help you get perspective—and to correct your attitude if need be. Pray, pray, pray—for wisdom, self-control, and for Him to increase your heart for her.

Remember the old adage, "Hurt people, hurt people, and are easily hurt."

Needy People

Not all Girls—but most—will tend to be needy for your attention. A wise lady once asked me, "Do you know the difference between a needy woman and one who isn't? One is getting her needs met."

These Girls have God-given needs that haven't been met—most of them will be starved for them. The *need to be loved* is the greatest. Then there is the need to belong, and the need to be in fellowship.

As she chooses to believe the truth about who she is, you can begin to ask her to start receiving again. Because people—including yourself—have been trying to fill those needs, but she chooses not to receive it, which is usually a self-worth issue. We want to change that with the truth of God, by being His hands and feet and loving her.

Try to see the end from the beginning. God took me from a meth addict to a ministry leader. He took David from a shepherd to a king. Imagine what he can do with her!

You may feel like the life and joy is being sucked out of you. Some Girls will try and make you feel guilty for not answering *every* time. It's never enough time spent with them. They ask ***you*** every question—not God.

Make sure you are staying filled up when working with this type of Girl—come full of the Holy Spirit. Don't try dealing with her alone and in the flesh…because in her unhealthiness she will win. And in that, she loses—and so do you. Take Jesus with you. Pray for strength and wisdom—before, during, and after—KNOW that you are not her Healer, Jesus is. You are His hands and feet.

You Win Some, You Lose Some

When I start mentoring a Girl, I tell her: "I won't leave you. You can leave me, but I won't leave you." If there is going to be a break in the relationship—she has to be the one to walk away, not me.

> I have a Girl who I've known for many years now; she was one of my closest Girls. Throughout years of mentoring and relationship building, hurts had happened, which she had not forgiven me for. I apologized, and asked forgiveness several times to no avail.
>
> We used to talk multiple times a week, and even several times a day, when she was going through a hard time. All of that ended, when she didn't forgive me and on top of that, I confronted her about a situation in her life and she didn't like my advice and did not want to be accountable to me.
>
> It hurt me on so many levels, and I miss her terribly, but I had to let her walk away. I can't make her want to be in a relationship with me. I can't help someone who won't let me. My hope and prayer is that she will come back someday, and

we can resume our relationship—because it's really hard to let go after so much time and heart was invested.

**I'm happy to report that just before publishing this book, *she contacted me*, and our relationship is on the mend now. Thank you, Jesus!

Your Girl may leave for a while, and then come back around. This is where you learn to hold her loosely and trust the Lord with her.

There are so many different reasons why a Girl may decide to walk away from you. Sometimes it's your fault, and sometimes they are convicted with how they are living and don't want to stop.

If it is possible, as far as it depends on you,
live *at peace with everyone.*

—Romans 12:18

There is no condemnation in Christ (Romans 8:1).

During the course of your mentoring years you're going to blow it at some point. We all do. **No one expects you to be perfect, so don't put that standard on yourself either.** Do your best to make peace and make it right, but then choose to move on. Don't keep chasing a person who doesn't want your help anymore, because there are plenty more people who do.

Mentoring is not always easy and it doesn't always *feel* like a blessing. It is a huge commitment of time and heart. There will come a time where you will want to drop her and quit—because she is challenging you, and being an absolute pain. Don't feel bad for thinking it or feeling it. *It's very normal.*

Hard to Work With

I want to encourage you to commit to those you mentor for life...no backdoors. If she wants to leave, that's *her choice*, not yours. When I have a Girl that I struggle with, I ask the Lord for His eyes, His wisdom, and His long-suffering heart; then I recommit to her, because love is a choice, and we need to choose it—even when it's hard, *especially* when it's hard.

I have had several Girls who, at some point, I believed I hated, however they are my very close friends now, and I love them to pieces. This type of Girl is worth your time and effort, because the outcome of her life is amazing—plus, God uses her to bring out the ugly in *you*. So don't give up on her, because God didn't give up on you.

There may (most likely) be a time in your relationship with her that she will get on your nerves—she'll call you too much, challenge you, question you, and make you mad. But it is important to recognize the assignment that God has given you. *Pray for her*. This will soften your heart and change her. Also, ask the Lord to renew your compassion and reveal any wicked way in you. Don't leave her. Recommit to her. It will be worth it in the end. Learn to shut your mouth, and wait till she is ready to listen to what you have to say again.

Some Girls are high-maintenance, and it takes a lot more dedication, prayer, and a humble heart to work with them, but they are so darn worth it. Again, some of the toughest Girls I've worked with have turned out to be some of my best friends. I'm so glad I didn't give up on them like I wanted to.

I had to really pray through those types of relationships, because I wanted to quit so many times. I had to *see the end from the beginning* in order to continue. Hardcore Girls are hardcore for Jesus too. Angry Girls are very passionate truth-speakers for Jesus once they yield. Find her soft spot. And do your best not to be afraid of her or avoid her. Show her unconditional love and courage in the Spirit—face her and lead her.

A Perfect Example

I worked with a Girl who took just about all the patience I had. She used to run around with gangs, deal drugs, had extreme anger issues, and stubborn to the core. I wanted to give up so many times, but I chose to hang in there and I'm so grateful that I did. That Girl is one of my closest friends now, an intricate part of our ministry and even included on the front cover of this book.

Try asking her, "What is really hurting you?"

You are not alone in this. Get help from other mentors to pray over you and encourage you through this worthy journey.

Going Back

Be careful lest you be tempted. It's important to go back to the places we were delivered from and bring others out. No one can speak to them and encourage them like you can. Think back…wouldn't it have been nice if the one who helped you *could also relate to you*?

It's also important that you have someone praying for you as you enter into conversations or places that trigger you. "Cover me…I'm going in." For instance, when I am working with a Girl who is graphically describing her sexual past, I am praying in my head practically the whole time. Plus after I leave, sometimes I am being bombarded with images from my past *or maybe hers*.

If this happens to you, what do you need to do? First, pray that God would remove those images—protect you from the Enemy. Then begin praying for her healing, and thanking God for yours. Those images are being used by the Enemy to try and sway you from helping her or others like her. If you need more help, and that didn't work, then call a friend who can pray for you or ask your husband (if that is applicable) to pray when you get home. *However, don't share the details with the other person or they will see the same things you are seeing.* Just tell them that you are being hit with graphic sexual or evil thoughts, and need to be covered in prayer. That's usually all I have to do, and they cease.

Do not allow yourself to ponder these thoughts and images, or wonder why you are thinking them. Do not own them as your own thoughts. This is where taking ALL your thoughts captive comes into play.

"We demolish arguments and every pretension that sets itself up against the knowledge of God, and ***we take captive every thought to make it obedient*** *to Christ."*

— 2 Corinthians 10:5 (emphasis mine)

Coming from a particular background—and coming out of it—you will usually have one of two responses (or reactions) to Girls still struggling through or engaging in it.

- An open heart, skills to encourage, and an eager spirit to help
- Fear, avoidance, anger, and judgment

While you are still healing, it's okay *and even wise* to avoid Girls who are struggling with the same thing; you are only avoiding for a time, but always remember that God saved you for a reason. He had more in mind than you being comfortable, clean, or celibate. While you are holding back in order to heal fully, have someone else who's been free for longer work with that Girl.

Brothers and sisters, if someone is caught in a sin, you who live by the Spirit should restore that person gently. But watch yourselves, or you also may be tempted.

— Galatians 6:1

Coming to Conclusions

Enter into relationships with an open mind, try not to assume anything. It is hard, but you need to be careful not to come to your own conclusion too soon—*especially* when someone refers a Girl to you, tells you their story, and even gives you the reason why they are the way they are. Most times, it's just their opinion. It is okay to think to yourself "*okay maybe that is going on, but maybe not.*" This is why you need to **ask a lot of questions** and make sure you understand where your Girl is really coming from. Don't assume; rather, ***ask***.

Some women who refer their daughters or sisters have already come to conclusions like *her husband IS cheating* or *she is definitely being sex trafficked*. It's not always the case, but when someone loves someone else, they tend to make assumptions that are incorrect. Take their opinion into consideration, but don't take it as fact.

The Blame Game

People who are unhealthy and stuck in an area, especially bitterness or additions LOVE to blame others and not own their part. Make your Girl focus on herself and stop blaming everyone else. It's time her to focus on HERSELF, and forget about the others for now.

Keep steering her back to herself and her own issues:

- *Okay, but what about you?*
- *How have you contributed to the problems in this relationship*?

CHAPTER 8—PURELY HIS MINISTRY

Go therefore and make disciples of all the nations, baptizing them in the name of the Father and the Son and the Holy Spirit, teaching them to observe all that I commanded you.

— Matthew 28:19-20

About the Ministry

"*Purely His Ministry* is a non-profit Christian ministry for those desiring to...***radically follow Jesus***. We are passionate about seeing people *set free* from anything that holds them back from becoming ALL that God has uniquely called them to be. Motivated by this passion, we ***equip*** individuals, other ministries and churches with the tools needed to ***effectively mentor*** in small groups and one-on-one."

The leaders of Purely His used to be stuck and defined by our past mistakes and failings; we can relate to where a person is. We "get it." Our newfound freedom and life compels us to meet people right where they are—and invite them into our lives—while we encourage them to give their whole lives to Jesús, and get unstuck from anything in the way of that. *"Follow me, as I follow Christ."*

Instilling Hope—Encouraging Freedom—Inspiring Change

We're passionate about being ready and getting others ready to meet God face to face, because we believe that we are living in the end times. We want to teach people to go all-in now, so when He comes back, they will run to Him, and not shrink back in shame.

When a person is all-in with Jesus, this is how their life looks:

- They have an eternal perspective on life

- They are focused on others and their salvation and growth in Christ
- They are coachable and ever-growing
- They aren't living for this world and the praises of people
- They are set apart and different from those around them
- They have a fire inside of them that is not typical

Mentoring Groups

We have found that having people meet in a Purely His Mentoring Group with others who can relate, all coming from different backgrounds, but headed in the same direction—speeds the healing process…because of the authentic *relationship* aspect. All learning to live purely and solely for the Lord with *Him* being their first love, their top priority.

These groups are for encouragement, accountability, connecting, and teaching. The mentors are encouraged to *drop their mask* and in so doing, the group members will drop theirs. The group is being mentored and raised up, so that they will in return mentor others. A discipleship movement. We are taking serious what Jesus commanded us all to do, by reaching those in our circle of influences all over the world.

The purpose behind our mentoring groups is to go *ALL-In* with Jesus, and to "Get Unstuck" from anything standing in the way of that. Our goal is to encourage people toward an awesome relationship with Jesus, assisting them in healing from unresolved issues, and equipping them to serve the Lord boldly—by passing on to others all that they have learned.

Our groups provide a safe place to:

- Talk about uncomfortable issues
- Get free from bondages
- Be encouraged in the Lord
- Be accepted without judgment
- Be held accountable
- Make new friendships that last a lifetime

Our mentoring groups are unique. We do not have a specific demographic that we are targeting, because struggles aren't limited by age, occupation, or background. These groups thrive on diversity—people learn valuable lessons from others who have different experiences than themselves.

Our groups are diverse by design: everyone coming from different backgrounds, but all headed the same direction...becoming *Purely His*. All struggles are welcome—including but not limited to—pornography, drugs, alcohol, promiscuity, low self-esteem, poor body image, eating disorders, marital problems, anger issues, self-harm, anger toward God or the church, loneliness, abuse, abortions, rape, and divorce. There isn't anything we haven't heard before, and we believe wholeheartedly that there isn't any struggle that the Lord can't heal.

The 5-Step Process we have developed is universal. It works great for men, women, youth, and couples. Due to the sensitive nature of our conversations, however, we choose not to mix genders when we get to the personal issues. *This includes couples as well.*

We realize that the need is great, but we are focused on quality, not quantity. Space is limited to eight attendants, and the groups are closed once that number is reached. We ask people to make a commitment to meet with their group once a week for five months. What we do is strategic and purposeful; we need the most comfortable environment possible to be effective.

A Typical Group Session

Our groups are anything but typical…or predictable. While there is a curriculum for the mentors to follow, they will lean more on the direction of the Holy Spirit than the curriculum. We've been told by many group attendants that the atmosphere we create is different than anything out there. The discussions are raw and intense at times, because our mentors have a past and are encouraged to "drop their masks and keep it real." This sets the tone for the others to do the same. The group attendants are also encouraged to share their experiences with other members—*thus learning to mentor while being mentored.*

Everyone learns from each other and this speeds the healing process dramatically.

Each group will be unique, because the leaders and group attendants are unique. Some groups will be held in churches, office buildings, homes, parks, or through video conferencing. But the main things remain the main things.

We have chosen to use two leaders per group. This can be helpful for so many reasons: two different personalities and backgrounds for those in the group to relate to, always a cover if one of the leaders is sick, and they can hold each other accountable to what the word of God says, while keeping in touch with the group participants outside of class. We are stronger together than we are apart. True and lasting relationships are started and maintained as we make a commitment to each other for life. It's where we say to each other "you're not alone anymore—we're in this together." We are working toward becoming Purely His— mentorship that goes the distance.

We have written our own curriculum, which outlines the 5-Step process we use. They are encouraged to make contact with each other throughout the week. Because of the sensitive nature of the things discussed, these are closed groups. The same group stays together for five months as they heal and grow together. We anticipate lifelong relationships being produced, because they have connected in a deep way through this process.

The 5-Step process is the outline we use in our weekly group time. Each week there is a different relatable topic that is discussed to get the conversation started. The majority of time spent in group is focused on healing. Our schedule is also built to promote well-rounded authentic relationships. This includes a day to serve, and a fun night to bond. We encourage contact with group members outside of the regular group time.

The outline for a weekly group time:

- Prayer
- Read the weekly discussion topic
- A few questions will be asked of the group

- Open it up for discussion (most of the time is spent in discussion)
- Prayer
- Homework is assigned (small amount)

Our groups produce results, because we do more than just sit around and talk about issues—we confront them and work through them. It's the perfect atmosphere to unload baggage and leave it there, so the participants can leave lighter and healthier. We offer a very relational atmosphere.

Ongoing mentoring and support is offered throughout the week, and after the group has completed the five-month meeting time, they can continue to chat through a private Facebook page, small get-togethers, retreats, and large gatherings. We also encourage the members of the group to stay in these close relationships, because we believe in mentoring that goes the distance.

We are raising workers up from within the harvest—teaching them to go "ALL-IN" with Jesus while getting "UNSTUCK" from anything in the way of that. We equip them to reach those in their circle of influence.

These groups are not designed to replace church, Bible study, or counseling. For the best results, combine all of the resources you can.

Support & Training

The Bible tells us that the harvest is ripe, but the workers are few. In other words, there is an abundant "crop" of people who are ready to make Jesus their Lord, but there aren't enough willing or equipped workers to make that a reality. We as Christians—leaders included—are stuck in some area that is preventing us from moving forward in authentic freedom. People often find themselves paralyzed or ill-equipped to live out the calling on their life and that usually indicates an area that they are stuck. It's vital to continue growing by Getting Unstuck as situations arise, because we can only take people as far as we have ourselves have gone. For instance, if a person has failed in the past, even in ministry, that fear can hold them back from taking a risk again. In that case, our training would help that person realize the grace of God over that situation, encourage them to receive His forgiveness and then forgive themselves.

We at Purely His feel compelled to raise mentors up from within the harvest, and with effective tools, equip those currently mentoring.

The group attendants get the best available training, because they learn through personal experience. These groups are built to be duplicated. Upon completion of the five months, our hope is that new groups will be launched by those who just experienced it. That is how we see the discipleship movement progressing.

We have found that even though a mentor has gone through one of our mentoring groups as an attendee and been trained through our general and advanced training, they still seem to learn the most as they are leading a group of their own. We encourage our leaders to participate in the group by engaging in answering the questions and doing the assignments in the curriculum. They are always learning and healing at a deeper level.

We are willing to travel to your area to train new groups of potential mentors. To inquire more about that, visit our website www.purelyhisministry.com. All materials needed to facilitate the groups are provided. We also provide mentoring for group leaders in both personal and group issues. *Even mentors need mentoring*. We understand that running a group can be intimidating, and that's why our trainings and this book will include how to mentor in groups and one-on-one. Anyone can do it. Jesus commands us to do it and He NEVER tells us to do something that He hasn't equipped us to do. Leaders are the workers, and our focus is ***raising up workers from within the harvest.*** It takes a leader to raise up other leaders.

You're not alone in this process; we're here to help you continue to *walk it out*, because mentors need mentoring too.

Purely His has ongoing support and training for those who decide to lead a mentoring group or mentor one-on-one. Support will come in the form of retreats, larger gatherings, a private Facebook page, and video conferencing calls. We're in this together.

There is a private Mentor's Facebook Page set up to be a safe place for us to develop a Sisterhood of people who are currently mentoring. It's a place to pour out our hearts about real issues, connect to new people, be encouraged, and get advice. You will be invited to the page once you have gone through the application process. It's important that you and I have someone to talk through our stuff with, get encouraged, and be held accountable.

How?

Start a group in your area. Reach your circle of influence for Jesus.

Our Training Box includes:

- Training Guide
- Videos
- Practical tools
- Mentor Leader assigned to help you

Our Sisterhood or Band of Brothers in a Box includes:

- Group Discussion Guide
- Tools and handouts to go along with each step
- Journals
- Pens
- Name tags
- Videos
- Mentor Leader assigned to help you

CHAPTER 9—WHAT ARE YOU WAITING FOR?

The Problem

The biggest complaints I hear about church:

- *I feel judged*
- *It appears that they think they're better than me, and make sure that I know that too*
- *No one is real at church, everyone is fake*
- *No one talks to me*

The data shows two trends, often at crosscurrents. Adults are aware of their very real spiritual needs, yet they are increasingly dissatisfied with the church's attempt to meet those spiritual needs and are turning elsewhere.

"The early church leaders didn't have the things we now consider essential for our faith. They didn't have official church buildings, vision statements or core values. They had no social media, radio broadcasts or celebrity pastors. They didn't even have the completed New Testament. Christ-followers were often deeply misunderstood, persecuted and some gave their lives for their faith. Yet they loved and they served and they prayed and they blessed—and slowly, over hundreds of years, they brought the empire to its knees. **They did it through love**."

Do you desire comfort *so much* that you don't want to get messy in the trenches? What else are we here for? Jesus is coming back...and this is ***our whole purpose***.

Website Citation: https://www.barna.org/barna-update/culture/661-americans-divided-on-the-importance-of-church#.U2R0X_ldWQw

It's up to us to bridge the gap! Can you remember back to how it felt when you were new to the church, or to the things of God (unless you were raised in the church and don't know what it's like for a first-timer)? It's *very difficult* especially if you're in sin—and wanting to get out of that lifestyle. It appears that everyone is perfect and holy, while you sit there feeling ashamed, dirty, and out of place.

Be the change

Let's keep it real; a lot of churches in America are weak and lame. We need to quit sitting around judging about *what's wrong with our churches* and stop waiting for the leadership to change it. We need to decide to ***be the change***.

Our churches are only weak, because we the people have not yet taken a stand! We need to do our part. We need to be mentoring—not waiting for protocol, the right outfit, makeup, pastoral permission, or even to hear a special calling. You want a calling?

Here's your calling:

***Go and make disciples of all men**.... (Matthew 28:19)*

Because ***the harvest is ripe, but the workers are few....***
(Matthew 9:37)

Discipleship and mentoring is missing in our churches. We as God's chosen people need to bring it back! We need to stop clinging to our comfortable lives, and start loving people out of dangerous and hurtful lifestyles. *Love covers over a multitude of sins* (1 Peter 4:8).

Don't you want everything you've gone through to be used for His honor and glory? Don't you want people to learn from our mistakes and triumphs? I know I do. We're saving people both steps and heartaches. We mentor because we want to give away what has been given to us. We don't need to be perfect, just ***imperfectly perfect***. We can be effective mentors by the grace of God.

I'm not teaching anything new—just reminding people what Jesus already said. Who better to reach the broken and lost than those that can relate? *But someone needs to reach them first.*

How, then, can they call on the one they have not believed in? And how can they believe in the one of whom they have not heard? And how can they hear without someone preaching to them? And how can anyone preach unless they are sent?

—Romans 10:14-15

We are not doing this to build our ministry alone, but to strengthen the *church*. This is not just a Purely His thing—it's a *Jesus* thing!

We are Christians; so let's act like Christ would. Think about how Jesus dealt with the woman caught in adultery:

...and said to Jesus, "Teacher, this woman was caught in the act of adultery. In the Law Moses commanded us to stone such women. Now what do you say?" They were using this question as a trap, in order to have a basis for accusing him.

But Jesus bent down and started to write on the ground with his finger. When they kept on questioning him, he straightened up and said to them, "Let any one of you who is without sin be the first to throw a stone at her." Again he stooped down and wrote on the ground.

At this, those who heard began to go away one at a time, the older ones first, until only Jesus was left, with the woman still standing there. Jesus straightened up and asked her, "Woman, where are they? Has no one condemned you?"

"No one, sir," she said.

"Then neither do I condemn you," Jesus declared. "Go now and leave your life of sin."

— John 8:4-11

These Girls need us to get down on our knees in the sand for them. It is *His* grace and mercy that leads people to repentance (Romans 2:4). They are going to look into our eyes to see if they see *uncondi-*

tional love or *condemnation* in our eyes, which is what they expect to see. Let's surprise them with unconditional love!

Be the one to get down on one knee and write in the sand on their behalf.

A Message from Michelle

As I complete this book, I have been thinking to myself, "An author? Who *me*? I am the most unlikely to succeed." But I tell you what—I am *exactly* the kind of girl that the Lord loves to use, because then He gets the glory for my life. Let my example be a reminder to you that the Lord can and wants to use your life to help others too, no matter where you come from or who you were before.

"Brothers and sisters, think of what you were when you were called. Not many of you were wise by human standards; not many were influential; not many were of noble birth.

But God chose the foolish things of the world to shame the wise; God chose the weak things of the world to shame the strong.

God chose the lowly things of this world and the despised things—and the things that are not—to nullify the things that are, so that no one may boast before him."

— 1 Corinthians 1:26-29

We have a world to reach in a very short amount of time—your lifetime—so let's get busy about our Father's business. If we all start reaching those in our circle of influence, then just think of the significant impact we can make *together*.

I was *way on the outside* of my mentor's circle of influence, but she was able to relate to me on two tiny parts of my story, and was successful in connecting with me in relationship. She gave me a little hope that someday I could actually be healthy and God could use me.

The Lord took me, a meth addict to a ministry leader, and He used mentors to get me here. Never say *never*, because the Lord has such great plans for all of us. You never know who that Girl is going to be when God moves you to invest in them—like Him, see the end from the beginning.

Won't you join us in this discipleship movement? You don't need to be perfect, rather, imperfectly perfect. If you decide to become a Purely His mentor, you have our full support—but even if you choose not to be a part of our ministry, still choose to join this movement and go reach your circle of influence for Jesus. I look forward to hearing the stories of how you stepped out in faith and allowed Him to use *Your Story* to reach others for Him!

Many, many blessings to you and yours,
Michelle

